The Problem of Emotions in Societies

Jonathan H. Turner

Like any other valued resource, emotions are distributed unequally. This distribution
of emotions roughly corresponds to the shares of other kinds of resource that
members of various social classes possess. The level of positive and negative
emotional energy evident among members of different social classes has large
consequences for the viability of human societies. When a large majority of members
in diverse social classes have reservoirs of positive emotional energy, these emotions
work to legitimate macrostructures and to build people's commitments to societies.
When, however, significant numbers of persons in lower social classes, and at times
in middle to upper social classes as well, reveal reservoirs of negative emotional
energy, they are likely to de-legitimate key institutional systems and, under
specifiable conditions, mobilize collectively—often with violent outcomes. Thus,
emotions are at the core of both integrative and disintegrative forces in societies, and
when large reservoirs of negative emotional energy exist, they pose a problem for
societies.

Jonathan H. Turner is Distinguished Professor at the University of California,
Riverside and University Professor, University of California. He is primarily a
general theorist who has sought to develop general scientific theories on all facets of
human social organization. He is the author of 35 books and around 200 research
articles and chapters. This present book is an effort to extend his more theoretical
analyses of human emotions to problems stemming from stratification of societies.

Framing 21st Century Social Issues

The goal of this new, unique Series is to offer readable, teachable "thinking frames" on today's social problems and social issues by leading scholars. These are available for view on http://routledge.custom gateway.com/routledge-social-issues.html.

For instructors teaching a wide range of courses in the social sciences, the Routledge *Social Issues Collection* now offers the best of both worlds: originally written short texts that provide "overviews" to important social issues *as well as* teachable excerpts from larger works previously published by Routledge and other presses.

As an instructor, click to the website to view the library and decide how to build your custom anthology and which thinking frames to assign. Students can choose to receive the assigned materials in print and/or electronic formats at an affordable price.

The Problem of Emotions in Societies

Jonathan H. Turner

University of California, Riverside

Routledge
Taylor & Francis Group

NEW YORK AND LONDON

First published 2011
by Routledge
270 Madison Avenue, New York, NY 10016

Simultaneously published in the UK
by Routledge
2 Park Square, Milton Park, Abingdon, Oxon OX14 4RN

Routledge is an imprint of the Taylor & Francis Group, an informa business

© 2011 Taylor & Francis

The right of Jonathan H. Turner to be identified as author of this work has been asserted by him in accordance with sections 77 and 78 of the Copyright, Designs and Patents Act 1988.

Typeset in Adobe Garamond and Gill Sans by EvS Communication Networx, Inc.

Library of Congress Cataloging in Publication Data
Turner, Jonathan H.
The problem of emotions in societies / Jonathan H. Turner.
p. cm. — (Framing 21st century social issues)
Includes bibliographical references.
1. Emotions—Sociological aspects. 2. Emotions—Social aspects. I. Title.
HM1033.T86 2011
302'.1—dc22
2010033530

ISBN13: 978-0-415-89207-0 (pbk)
ISBN13: 978-0-203-83425-1 (ebk)

To:
Louis Bozzetti, M.D.
Again, thank you

Contents

Series Foreword

The world in the early 21st century is beset with problems—a troubled economy, global warming, oil spills, religious and national conflict, poverty, HIV, health problems associated with sedentary lifestyles. Virtually no nation is exempt, and everyone, even in affluent countries, feels the impact of these global issues.

Since its inception in the 19th century, sociology has been the academic discipline dedicated to analyzing social problems. It is still so today. Sociologists offer not only diagnoses; they glimpse solutions, which they then offer to policy makers and citizens who work for a better world. Sociology played a major role in the civil rights movement during the 1960s in helping us to understand racial inequalities and prejudice, and it can play a major role today as we grapple with old and new issues.

This series builds on the giants of sociology, such as Weber, Durkheim, Marx, Parsons, Mills. It uses their frames, and newer ones, to focus on particular issues of contemporary concern. These books are about the nuts and bolts of social problems, but they are equally about the frames through which we analyze these problems. It is clear by now that there is no single correct way to view the world, but only paradigms, models, which function as lenses through which we peer. For example, in analyzing oil spills and environmental pollution, we can use a frame that views such outcomes as unfortunate results of a reasonable effort to harvest fossil fuels. "Drill, baby, drill" sometimes involves certain costs as pipelines rupture and oil spews forth. Or we could analyze these environmental crises as inevitable outcomes of our effort to dominate nature in the interest of profit. The first frame would solve oil spills with better environmental protection measures and clean-ups, while the second frame would attempt to prevent them altogether, perhaps shifting away from the use of petroleum and natural gas and toward alternative energies that are "green."

These books introduce various frames such as these for viewing social problems. They also highlight debates between social scientists who frame problems differently. The books suggest solutions, both on the macro and micro levels. That is, they suggest what new policies might entail, and they also identify ways in which people, from the ground level, can work toward a better world, changing themselves and their lives and families and providing models of change for others.

Readers do not need an extensive background in academic sociology to benefit from these books. Each book is student-friendly in that we provide glossaries of terms for the uninitiated that are keyed to bolded terms in the text. Each chapter ends with questions for further thought and discussion. The level of each book is accessible to undergraduate students, even as these books offer sophisticated and innovative analyses.

In an unusual and imaginative treatment, Jonathan Turner considers the social problem of emotions—specifically, of the unequal distribution of emotions. Groups vary in the access they have to what Turner calls positive and negative emotions. He speculates about what happens when significant groups of people, especially at the bottom of social and economic strata, are negatively emotional—mad at the system. This is de-stabilizing, as we see today when vast numbers of Americans are mad at politicians in Washington and withdraw their legitimation of the democratic process.

Preface

Out-of-control emotions can be seen just about everywhere we look. In societies all over the world, including American society, individuals are angry and willing to engage in violence or they are feeling great sadness or fear. As I seek to emphasize in this short volume, human emotionality is both basic to us as an evolved feature of our genome; and yet at the same time, emotions represent a very large problem for human societies, especially as they have grown and become more stratified. Humans are the most emotional animals on earth, and so violence fueled by the arousal of anger should not be surprising, nor should the problems that come with fear and sadness be seen as abnormal. We are wired to be emotional, and thus under certain sociocultural conditions, the arousal of negative emotions and violence is inevitable. Even emotions that are not violent, such as alienation, sadness, and despair, are problematic for societies because they signal a lack of commitment to the social structures and their cultures that make social life possible. Thus, the arousal of negative emotions in general can become a problem for societies.

At first it may take a mind shift to visualize emotions as a resource, and as such, they are like any other resource and, hence, are distributed unequally to people in societies. Positive emotions are a highly valued resource because they give people pleasure and the confidence to secure additional types of resource—whether money, power, influence, prestige, or just about any other resource that is valued. In contrast, negative emotions are punishing because they cause individual pain and often keep them from gaining access to other valued resources.

Like any other resource that is unequally distributed, emotions are stratified. Those in higher social classes are more likely to possess a surplus of positive emotional energy, whereas those in lower social classes are more likely to feel higher levels of negative emotional energy. Thus, this distribution of emotions roughly corresponds to the shares of others kinds of resources that members of various social classes possess. The level of positive and negative emotional energy evident among members of different social classes has, as noted above, large consequences for the viability of human societies. When a large majority of members in diverse social classes have reservoirs of positive emotional energy, these emotions work to legitimate macrostructures and to build people's commitments to societies. When, however, significant numbers of persons in lower social classes, and at times in middle to upper social classes as well, reveal reservoirs of negative emotional energy, they are likely to de-legitimate key institutional systems and, under specifiable conditions, mobilize collectively—often with violent outcomes. Emotions are, therefore, at the core of both integrative and disintegrative forces in societies, and when large reservoirs of negative emotional energy exist, they pose a problem for societies.

The dynamics of emotion are, however, complicated because humans have the capacity to feel rather complex sets of emotions. Moreover, they often repress unpleasant emotions, removing them from consciousness. Yet, repression only makes the dynamics of emotion more complex and potentially more problematic for societies because repressed emotions intensify and often transmute into even more negative emotional states. So, even as persons in societies try to remove emotions from consciousness, they are often raising the emotional stakes and making the problem of emotions even more severe.

1: Why are Humans So Emotional?

❧

"The world has gone mad!" "People are crazy!" and other such phrases are often uttered when individuals and groups do things that seem, well ... "crazy." These and many similar phrases point to an obvious but surprisingly little-studied topic: emotions and how they affect the organization of human societies. We tend to become folk psychologists when thinking about emotions, seeing them as affective states that individuals experience and express. There is an obvious truth to this psychological bias because emotions are ultimately generated in our brains, below the large neo-cortex that allows for language and culture. At the same time, however, emotions are what hold societies together or, as is often the case, tear them down. Emotions and their effects on society are thus worthy topics of inquiry.

The Origins of Human Emotionality

Humans are probably the most emotional animals on earth (Turner 1996a, 1996b, 1999, 2000). We can experience a wide variety of emotions of wildly varying intensities. And we react emotionally to almost every situation, even if we are only dimly aware of our feelings. Moreover, we can repress unpleasant emotions, only to have them reappear in confused emotional displays that can disrupt not only our personal well-being but also social relations and even society. There is a reason for humans' emotionality: our primate ancestors—often termed **hominids** or **hominins**—needed to become more emotional or die. It is this dramatic enhancement of our ancestors' emotional capacities that allowed them to become better organized and that today, even in the very large societies, holds societies together. If our hominid ancestors had not become emotional, you and I would not be here.

We often think of the great apes—our closest living relatives—as highly social and gregarious. But, in their natural habitats, they are not. Apes are surprisingly individualistic, promiscuous, mobile, and weak-tie animals whose groups are temporary and constantly changing as they break apart and reform (Maryanski 1996b, 1997). Such behaviors were well adapted to animals that evolved in the sparse, terminal feeding areas high in the arboreal habitat or forests of Africa 20 million years ago. In this difficult set of niches, there was not enough space or food to sustain large, stable groups composed of big mammals. While it is somewhat embarrassing to admit, monkeys, who are not as strong or smart as apes, won the battle for the best feeding areas in the arboreal habitat. For, in a true Darwinian competition, monkeys took over the core regions of the trees in Africa where there was both space and enough food to form larger, more stable groups. The result was for apes to be pushed to terminal feeding areas of trees. It is in these niches at the tops of trees that apes developed the characteristics that make us human: greater intelligence; strong shoulders, arms, and wrists; sensitive and dexterous fingers; and abilities to brachiate (rotate the arm 360 degrees). The one thing that apes could not do in this dangerous area where one false step would mean death by gravity is organize large and stable groups. Thus, unlike most mammals, humans do not have herding, pod, pack, pride, troop, or group organizational tendencies built into our genome (Maryanski 1992, 1993, 1996a; Maryanski and Turner 1992; Turner 2000; Turner and Maryanski 2008). To organize, humans must rely on alternative mechanisms, and the most important of these bonding mechanisms is emotions.

You may think that this description of our ancestors has little relevance to the big problems of human societies today, but it does. Millions of years ago, the forests of Africa began to recede, causing the spread of the great open-country grasslands of the savanna. As the trees began to disappear, so did the habitat of both monkeys and apes, forcing many to the ground in a desperate effort to survive. Monkeys were much better equipped for life on the African savanna because they are very well organized, with dominance hierarchies among males and lineages of related females. The result is that savanna-dwelling monkeys can march across dangerous open-country grasslands in almost militaristic fashion, making it difficult for predators to pick them off. In contrast, apes never had tight-knit groups; on the savanna, therefore, they were sitting ducks because they could not organize naturally for defense or food foraging, especially as they were forced to leave the forests permanently and survive in predator-ridden open-country conditions. The result was carnage, leading to the mass extinction of most species of apes. Indeed, humans and our handful of close relatives—orangutans, chimpanzees (two species), and gorillas (two species)—are all that is left of the ape line that is close to us, although there are several species of smaller gibbons and siamangs that are very distant relatives to humans. And none of these species of present-day apes can survive outside the forests. Only humans among the hundreds and probably thousands of species of apes that once lived can survive on the savanna. Somehow our hominid ancestor beat the odds and got better organized; and this occurred because natural selection hit upon a solution to the weak-tie, loose organization of apes: make apes more emotional so that they can form new kinds of affect-driven social relations that would become the basis for more cohesive patterns of social organization.

Emotions are, however, a double-edged sword; they bring us together but they also can push us apart. They make us violent, willing to kill our own kind in many different ways, ranging from murder through war to genocide, and lots of other ways of killing people. Emotions arouse us to the point of being willing to tear societies apart in riots and revolutions. They alienate us from others, groups, organizations, and societies. They lead us to say unkind things or even to be violent against loved ones. Emotions are thus volatile, despite our reliance on them to love others, to form friendships, and to feel the wonderful solidarity of cohesive groups. Emotions make us happy and give us pleasure, but they also make us sad, depressed, fearful, angry, righteous, and vengeful. Emotions cause many problems for people and societies, and yet we need them to form bonds and attachments to each other and to social structures, from small groupings to whole societies. They are, therefore, a topic that we need to know more about, if we are understand ourselves and the social world around us.

The Range of Human Emotions

The human palate of emotional states is built from a few **primary emotions**, or emotions that are hard-wired into our neuro-anatomy. Much like the many shades of colors that can be blended from a few primary colors (Plutchik 1980), humans can feel and express a much larger palate of emotions, and we can also read this palate of emotions in the gestures of others. Human neurology is, of course, far more complex than a color wheel, but the analogy makes the critical point: humans are hard-wired in their brains to experience and express a few primary emotions, as are all other mammals. But compared with all other mammals, even highly intelligent ones with large brains, humans can also mix many new emotional colors from a relatively small number of primary emotions. What are these primary emotions? Well, it is embarrassing to say that there is not complete consensus on which emotions are primary, but all researchers and theorist would agree on this much: the four emotions of *anger, fear, sadness,* and *happiness* are primary. Some scholars add several more emotions such as *disgust, surprise, expectancy,* and a few others. But all agree on these four, and this is enough to tell the story of emotions (Turner 2000: 68–69; Turner and Stets 2005: 15–16). In humans and, to a lesser degree in some intelligent mammals, these primary emotions vary by degree of intensity and valence. Table 1.1 represents my best effort, drawing from others, to use words to communicate the range of affective states of each of these primary emotions (Turner 2000, 2007a). For each primary emotion, the valence of the emotion goes from a low- through moderate- to high-intensity state.

Another feature of Table 1.1 should stand out: three of these four primary emotions are *negative* and work against social bonding. People who are angry invite counter-anger; those who are fearful are usually avoided; and the same is true for people who are sad. Only the satisfaction–happiness continuum reveals positive emotions that can be used to forge bonds in the absence of genetically driven bioprogrammers for group formation. Thus, the majority of primary emotions that humans experience are negative and generally work against forming social ties and groups revealing solidarity. The same is true for most intelligent mammals but unlike humans they have built in programmers to form packs, prides, pods, troops, and herds. As a consequence, they

Table 1.1 Variants of Primary Emotions

	Low intensity	Moderate intensity	High intensity
Satisfaction–happiness	content sanguine serenity gratified	cheerful buoyant friendly amiable enjoyment	joy bliss rapture jubilant gaiety elation delight thrilled exhilarated
Aversion–fear	concern hesitant reluctance shyness	misgivings trepidation anxiety scared alarmed unnerved panic	terror horror high anxiety
Assertion–anger	annoyed agitated irritated vexed perturbed nettled rankled piqued	displeased frustrated belligerent contentious hostility ire animosity offended consternation	dislike loathing disgust hate despise detest hatred seething wrath furious inflamed incensed outrage
Disappointment–sadness	discouraged downcast dispirited	dismayed disheartened glum resigned gloomy woeful pained dejected	sorrow heartsick despondent anguished crestfallen

Source: Data from Turner 2007a.

do not have to rely so much on emotions as humans (and our distant ancestors) to create and sustain social structures, from groups to large-scale societies. How, then, did natural selection get around this major obstacle of negative emotions?

The neurology of the subcortical areas of the human brain, where emotions are ultimately generated, has been rewired in significant ways from our closest primate relatives; and so this wiring probably has something to do with answering the above question. Here is a bit of speculation on my part, but still a reasonable conjecture in light of how the brain is structured to produce emotions (for details, see Turner 2000). Somehow the human brain was rewired in ways that allows for the combining of primary emotions into what can be called **first-order elaborations** of primary emotions

(Plutchik 1962). What this wiring seems to do is mix—to be metaphorical about what obviously is a complex process—a greater amount of one primary emotion with a lesser amount of another primary emotion. The result is a much larger palate of emotions beyond those denoted in Table 1.1. At the same time, this mixing of emotions generates new kinds of affective states that, in many cases, blunt the power of negative emotions alone. In Table 1.2, the primary emotion listed in bold type represents the more dominant emotion that is mixed (denoted by a + sign) with a lesser amount of another primary emotion (denoted by italics). At the right, the new and dramatically expanded palate of emotions generated by this kind of mixing are listed. For example, a greater amount of satisfaction–happiness mixed with a lesser amount of aversion–fear produces emotions such as *wonder, hopeful, relief, gratitude, pride,* and *reverence*; all of these emotions blunt the power of fear alone and, moreover, produce emotions that can promote social bonding. Indeed, wonder and reverence can promote attachment to religious beliefs and the pantheon of supernatural beings and/or forces, thereby moralizing emotions in cultural beliefs and invoking powerful beings and forces that can exercise social control. To take another example, a greater amount of assertion–anger mixed with aversion–fear produces emotions such as *suspiciousness, abhorrence,* and *jealousy,* which hardly promote positive bonding but, even in these cases, the power of intense anger alone is blunted and turned into emotions that can be used as negative sanctions that are less intense than anger by itself.

By reading the emotions on the right side of Table 1.2, it is easy to see increased nuance in human emotions, compared with other mammals, including highly intelligent primates. Moreover, in most cases happiness mixed with one of the negative emotions produces emotions that are more likely to promote social bonding, although there are exceptions. For instance, anger mixed with happiness produces powerful emotions like *vengeance,* where people are happy to use their anger to harm others. Indeed, the emotion behind murder, terrorism, gang-banging, or genocide is often vengeance; and so we must remember that expanding the palate of human emotions remains a double-edge sword: many more associative emotions are generated to overcome the power of the three negative emotions alone, but some incredibly powerful and destructive emotions are also produced. Thus, it is these destructive emotions that are at the core of the title of this book, *The Problem of Emotions in Societies,* as we will see in later chapters. And yet, this first-order combination of emotions listed in Table 1.2 was essential to our ancestors' survival as natural selection grabbed onto subcortical areas of the brain to make these proto-human ancestors sufficiently emotional to form social bonds so that they could become more organized and, hence, more able to survive in open-country savanna conditions. Indeed, without this enhancement of our ancestors' emotionality, they would have become extinct like all other savanna-dwelling apes. So, we will have to live with the danger of using emotions to overcome very weak bioprogrammers for group formation in hominids and in humans today.

With the neurology for first-order elaborations of emotions, natural selection had

Table 1.2 First-Order Elaborations of Primary Emotions

SATISFACTION–HAPPINESS

Satisfaction–happiness + *aversion–fear*	*produces* ——▶	wonder, hopeful, relief, gratitude, pride, reverence
Satisfaction–happiness + *assertion–anger*	*produces* ——▶	vengeance, appeased, calmed, soothed, relish, triumphant, bemused
Satisfaction–happiness + *disappointment–sadness*	*produces* ——▶	nostalgia, yearning, hope

AVERSION–FEAR

Aversion–fear + *satisfaction–happiness*	*produces* ——▶	awe, reverence, veneration
Aversion–fear + *assertion–anger*	*produces* ——▶	revolted, repulsed, antagonism, dislike, envy
Aversion–fear + *disappointment–sadness*	*produces* ——▶	dread, wariness

ASSERTION–ANGER

Assertion–anger + *satisfaction–happiness*	*produces* ——▶	condescension, mollified, rudeness, placated, righteousness
Assertion–anger + *aversion–fear*	*produces* ——▶	abhorrence, jealousy, suspiciousness
Assertion–anger + *disappointment–sadness*	*produces* ——▶	bitterness, depression, betrayed

DISAPPOINTMENT–SADNESS

Disappointment–sadness + *satisfaction–happiness*	*produces* ——▶	acceptance, moroseness, solace, melancholy
Disappointment–sadness + *aversion–fear*	*produces* ——▶	regret, forlorn, remorseful, misery
Disappointment–sadness + *assertion–anger*	*produces* ——▶	aggrieved, discontent, dissatisfied, unfulfilled, boredom, grief, envy, sullenness

something to select on and produce what are probably the most important emotions for maintaining social order in human groupings: *shame* and *guilt*. Most scholars who study primates agree that even those great apes closest to humans do not experience shame and guilt; and so, from the rewiring for first-order emotions (combining two primary emotions), natural selection hit upon a further solution to the precarious-ness of using emotions to forge social bonds. Selection rewired the brain to produce **second-order elaborations** of primary emotions, such as **shame**, **guilt**, and **alien-ation**, by mixing the three negative emotions. Shame is the emotion of feeling inad-equate and small because one has not met expectations (norms) for how to behave in a situation. This is one of the most powerful emotions of social control because it is so painful to persons, which motivates them to avoid experiencing shame or to make amends to others when shamed. Shame varies along a continuum of intensity, from *embarrassment* at the low end to moderate *shame* to high-intensity *humiliation*. Can there be a more painful emotion than humiliation in the eyes of oneself and others? And so, people work very hard to avoid shame, even low-intensity variants like embarrassment. Thus, shame is the emotion of social control because a person and others around this person are always monitoring behaviors to see if expectations have been met; and if they have not, persons will experience shame as they assess their competence, and others will also use negative sanctions laced with emotions ranging from *disappointment* through *sadness* to a first-order elaboration like *righteous anger* at the high-intensity end, or they may use *anger* alone and one of its variants. The key point is that we are all aware of how we are doing in reference to expectations in a situation, as are others. And, when we monitor ourselves and find that we have not lived up to expectations, we will experience a variant of shame; and if others are present to see our failure, we will experience a more intense variant of shame, especially if expectations are important or even moral to persons.

Guilt is the other emotion of social control. We experience guilt when we perceive or are told by others that we have not lived up to moral codes of right–wrong, good–bad, appropriate–inappropriate, and other labels that define morality. Moral codes are powerful because they have emotions attached to them, such as *pride* and *happiness* when codes are obeyed and emotions like *guilt* for self and *righteous anger* (from others) when actions of a person have violated moral codes. Much like shame, guilt is a painful emotion, although probably not as intensely painful as shame, but still painful. Indeed, guilt can affect us for a long time, and so humans try to avoid experiencing it. And, they are highly motivated to make amends in their own eyes but, equally important, in the eyes of others to absolve their sense of guilt.

Without the capacity to experience shame and guilt, human social organization could not exist, as we know it. However, like all emotions, shame and guilt have a dark side; they can generate extreme pathologies in a person when consistently experienced. For example, when a father or mother has consistently imposed negative sanctions on their child, this child will have had to endure constant shame and perhaps guilt as well; and in all likelihood, this child will exhibit behavioral pathologies such as diffuse *anger*, *anxiety*, and *depression*, as an adult. As we will outline in the next chapter, because shame is so painful, individuals often repress it, and once repressed it increases in intensity but is often transmuted to another negative emotion, with *diffuse anger* being a common emotion arising from repressed shame. As a result, a shamed person will often be an angry individual who disrupts social relations and, if acting collectively with others, can disrupt social structures and, at times, whole societies. Indeed, as we will see in Chapter IV, repressed shame and the transmuted emotion of anger that emerges is often the emotional force behind extreme violence in human societies (Scheff 1988, 1997; Scheff and Retzinger 1991; Turner 2007b). And so, like all emotions, shame and to a lesser extent guilt are, once again, a double-edged sword; they promote self-monitoring and motivate conformity to normative expectations and moral codes, but they can, when repressed, cause behavioral pathologies as well as violence.

Table 1.3 Rank-ordering of Constituent Primary Emotions of Shame, Guilt, and Alienation

	1	2	3
Shame	disappointment–sadness (at self)	assertion–anger (at self)	aversion–fear (at consequences for self)
Guilt	disappointment–sadness (at self)	aversion–fear (at consequences for self)	assertion–anger (at self)
Alienation	disappointment–sadness (at self)	assertion–anger (at situation/others)	aversion–fear (at consequences for self)

Why would shame in particular and at times guilt as well become so prominent in humans? The answer resides in how natural selection was rewiring the immediate ancestors to humans. Shame and guilt, it can be speculated, represent one more way of turning the three negative primary emotions into emotions that promote social order. In Table 1.3, the structure of shame and guilt is outlined—granted, in a highly speculative manner. These are, as noted above, second-order elaborations because they take the three negative primary emotions and convert them into a composite negative emotion—shame or guilt—that works to promote the social order. Once natural selection took the route of combining primary emotions to increase the ability to form social bonds, perhaps shame and guilt would inevitably emerge. These are the most powerful emotions of social control in human groupings because they are very painful and thus motivate people to behave in accordance with norms and moral codes and to make amends when they transgress from norms and moral codes. Yet, their underlying structure reveals why they would have a dark side, especially if repressed, intensified, and transmuted into one of the constituent negative emotions that make up shame—that is, sadness, anger, or fear.

Another second-order elaboration is *alienation*, or the sense of disaffection from others, social structures, and their cultures. Alienated people are not motivated to invest in social relations or social structures; they desire to be elsewhere but often cannot, and so they maintain their distance. Alienation is not like shame and guilt, but can accomplish two things. First, it mitigates the power of the three negative emotions when expressed alone. Second, it tells others that there is a tear in the social fabric and, perhaps, moves them to be more inclusive and to bring the alienated person back into the social fold. Alienation is thus a signal to others to try and do something about a disaffected and unhappy person. Alienation can also cause a group or even a whole society to collapse, if enough people are alienated and unmotivated to abide by the rules and to participate in key social structures. So, like any combination of negative emotions, the negative potential alienation for society is always present.

Table 1.3 speculates that shame, guilt, and alienation are built from the three negative emotions mixed together with varying levels of intensity. All three of these emotions are, it is hypothesized, built from a greater amount of disappointment–sadness mixed with lesser amounts of aversion–fear and assertion–anger. In their relative rank-order of intensity, shame is mostly disappointment–sadness, followed in relative intensity by anger (at self) and fear (of the consequences to self) of having not met expectations of others in a situation. Alienation reveals the same structure but the anger component is directed more at the situation than self. And, guilt reverses the rank-ordering of intensity of anger and fear, thus being an emotion composed of mostly disappointment-sadness followed by fear (of the consequences to self) and anger (at self). This simple shift in the relative portions of anger and fear produces very different emotions which, if we think about it, is a rather efficient way to mitigate the power of the three negative emotions alone and, at the same time, generate powerful emotions of social control for animals like humans who are still, at their neurological core, weak-tie apes.

This structure helps us understand the outcome of situations where either shame or guilt is repressed, a topic to be taken up in more detail in the next chapter. Any of the three constituent negative emotions can emerge from repression, intensification, and transmutation, but the second emotion is the most likely to emerge. Thus, in the case of shame, *anger* is likely to surface for repressed shame, although *depression* and *anxiety* are also possible. Repressed shame can also produce episodes where one, then another, and still another of the three negative emotions emerge. Situations can often determine which of the negative emotions will be emitted. But, for the purposes of exploring the problem of emotions in human societies, it is when anger—indeed, intense and *diffuse anger*—emerges that problems for societies arise, especially if large numbers of individuals have experienced and repressed shame, only to have it emerge as anger that can fuel collective violence.

In the case of repressed guilt, *fear* in the form of an anxiety disorder is the most likely outcome of repression, intensification, and transmutation, although both *sadness* as depression or *anger* can also be felt. Still, chronically guilty persons who have repressed much of this guilt will typically manifest one of many anxiety disorders (for example, phobias, obsessive–compulsive disorders), just as chronically shamed persons are most likely to reveal diffuse and often intense anger. While diffuse anger and anxiety are painful, and especially so when they disrupt social relations, they are less painful than shame and guilt that cannot be resolved. When people are placed in situations where they chronically experience shame or guilt, some repression is highly likely, particularly when these situations are encountered when a person is young and cannot escape the actions of self and others that cause them to experience these emotions. And, if enough persons experience and repress these emotions, the transmuted emotions that emerge, particularly those for shame, can pose problems of social control in a society.

Conclusion

Humans are emotional because we need emotions to form social bonds that can build social structures. We are not like most other mammals that have bioprogrammers that push them to form group structures. All mammals reveal at least four primary emotions, although a few additional primary emotions are hypothesized by various researchers (see Turner and Stets 2005: 15–16 for a list of various typologies of primary emotions). Despite different formulations, all scholars agree that anger, fear, sadness, and happiness are neurologically wired into mammals and certainly humans. Three of these primary emotions are negative, and so the big obstacle for natural selection, operating blindly on the neurology of human's private ancestors, was to convert these negative emotions into ones that would promote bonding. This was apparently accomplished by re-wiring the subcortical areas of the brain and the connections between these areas and the very large human neo-cortex (where language, culture, and thinking occur) to generate new varieties of emotions that could be used to form social bonds. Initially, the variety of primary emotions was expanded by natural selection, then first-order elaborations of two primary emotions evolved, and finally second-order elaborations combining the three negative emotions into shame, guilt, and alienation were built by natural selection into human neuroanatomy. In this way, the hominid ancestors of humans were able to forge stronger social bonds, and today it is only because of emotions that humans are able to forge bonds of solidarity and develop commitment to social structures and their cultures. Yet, first-order elaborations of emotions like *vengeance* or transmuted second-order elaborations like *diffuse anger* or *high anxiety* work against social order, and in essence, are the price that humans must pay for using emotions to build social structures. Moreover, other second-order elaborations like *alienation* reduce commitments to social structures and culture, thus decreasing their viability.

The problem of emotions in human societies almost always involves some of the dark side of our emotional palate. Negative emotions produce many behavioral pathologies, but they do more: when groups and subpopulations of persons must chronically experience negative emotions, the range of problems for a society increases dramatically, often to the point of destroying the social order—as we will see in Chapter IV. For the time being, let us consider some of the implications of what we know about human emotions thus far.

DISCUSSION QUESTIONS

1. Is it really true that humans, as evolved apes, are comparatively low sociality animals?
2. Why do people prefer to text rather than talk with others on the phone? Is this preference related to humans' ape core as a weak-tie animal?
3. Do you feel engulfed with too much interaction? And, do you find yourself trying to escape situations where you become too engaged?
4. Why is social interaction among humans so animated? And tiring?
5. Why are emotions so hard to control? What does this mean for how we must act in group contexts?
6. When people "lose it" emotionally, what happens and how do others respond?
7. What would happen to a society where people became too emotional, or not emotional enough?

II: The Dark Side of Emotions

~~~

There are areas of the brain below the neo-cortex that hold "unconscious memories." Some of these unconscious memories are the result of **repression**, or pushing experiences that have aroused negative emotions about self below the level of consciousness. It may seem strange to bring this great insight by early psycho-analysts like Sigmund Freud into a discussion of emotions and society, but repression of such emotions as *shame* and *guilt*, plus any other emotional experiences that attack a person's sense of self, is quite common because these emotions are painful and difficult to live with. And, when large numbers of people in society must cope with unpleasant emotions and when they have even experienced a sense of collective shame, these emotions are inevitably going to have more than just consequences for the mental health of a single person. They can, under certain conditions, cause mobilization for extreme violence or for withdrawal of legitimacy from the core institutions of a society, perhaps the whole society itself. This dark and hidden side of people's emotional well-being can thus have large effects on all people in a society.

Repression as the Master Defense Mechanism

What is Repression?

One reason for the power of repressed emotions is, as emphasized in the last chapter, that repression of negative emotions often leads to the intensification of the emotions over time and, then, to their transmutation into a new emotion. In the case of shame, any of its three constituent negative emotions is possible but *diffuse anger* is the potentially most volatile. This repression–intensification–transmutation sequence is a general process, with repression being the master defense mechanism, or the cognitive processes that push highly painful negative emotions from consciousness. A person may or may not remember the experience that caused the arousal of painful emotions, but the emotions will, to varying degrees, be pushed below the level of consciousness. If they just went away, these defense mechanisms would be most useful to a person, but the emotions persist and build in intensity and re-emerge as a emotion that is more acceptable to self—although the new emotion may be harmful to a person's long-run mental health and relations with others. And, as we see, such emotions can be harmful to the very social structures essential for the operation of a society.

What are Defense Mechansims?

A **defense mechanism** is any cognitive dynamic that protects self from the full experience of negative emotions. These defense mechanisms operate at many levels and involve varying degrees of repression. Let me list these mechanisms under two levels of repression: (1) **defensive strategies** and (2) **secondary defense mechanisms**.

Defensive Strategies

Oftentimes, individuals do not have to engage in high levels of repression; instead, they employ interpersonal and cognitive strategies to protect themself (McCall and Simmons 1978; Turner 2007a: 93–95). Let me only quickly review them.

Selective perception is a defensive strategy that enables a person to see a situation in a way that protects self, without high degrees of repression. For example, a person may interpret gestures and actions of others toward self as being playful when in fact the emotions directed at self by another are actually quite hostile and negative. Like most defensive strategies, these can be effective in the short run, but if they are consistently employed at any time when negative emotions are directed at a person, then the repression is more intense and will activate ancillary defense mechanism discussed below. The same is true for all defensive strategies; they do not work well after a time if habitually employed, because others get irritated and begin to direct even more negative emotions—*frustration, irritation, outrage,* and other forms of *anger*—which will only force more repression to a point where ancillary defense mechanisms must be activated.

Selective interpretation is related to selective perception, but involves putting an interpretative twist on the signals emitted by others so as to protect self. For instance, a male may have made a romantic "hit" on a woman in a situation in which any bystander would interpret her reaction as a demonstrative rejection, but the man in this *faux pas* interprets the gesture as "playing hard to get" in an attempt to hide her true romantic feelings from him—a formula for further rejection and the need for even more selective perception that can only lead to emotional and interpersonal trouble.

Disavowals revolve around questioning the credibility or the importance of the others who have aroused negative emotions. Individuals also protect their sense of self by disavowing a behavior that has brought a negative emotional reaction from others as "not being myself" which serves as an apology to others while protecting self from the full impact of shame. A more serious disavowal comes when a person rejects the other(s) or audience that has reacted negatively to the behaviors of a person, seeing them as not "qualified" or as not "important." Blowing off an audience will, in the end, only increase their negative responses toward a person, but in the short term self has been protected.

Short-term credit draws upon past experience where positive emotions have been aroused in a particular type of situation in order to "ride out" an episode where more negative emotions have emerged. When individuals have a legacy of successful performances in situations, the failure to meet expectations can be defined as simply a lapse (a version of disavowal), but the person does not reject the audience and may even offer a "not being myself" kind of apology. Rather, this person simply rides out the episode of negative emotions by invoking memories—stored like an account in a bank, in this case a cognitive memory bank—that recall all of the other times that this individual was successful in the current situation, drawing from this account some short-term emotional credit. Obviously, if the negative emotions persist in this situation in the future, then this strategy will not work; instead, it will lead to cognitive and emotional bankruptcy, and force a person to use more powerful defense mechanism.

These kinds of defensive strategies are, in essence, quick fixes to awkward situations that might cause negative emotions about self. If used only sporadically, they will not harm individuals and their social relations. If, however, these are used chronically, they will only arouse more negative reactions from others and, in the end, force a person to experience highly negative feelings about themselves. Most of the time for most people, these strategies are used infrequently; and as a consequence, individuals are able to smooth over a problematic situation and protect self from negative emotional experiences. But, if used too often and if they begin to be counterproductive as others react more negatively to a person, then a higher level of repression must be invoked, plus additional ancillary defense mechanisms.

Secondary Defense Mechanisms

After repression, additional defense mechanisms will operate to transmute the repressed emotion(s) and channel them toward somewhat different targets. There are other defense mechanisms besides repression, although repression is the master defense mechanism. Table 2.1 lists these secondary defense mechanisms that transmute the repressed emotions and most importantly target these emotions toward social objects, as is indicated in the right-hand column of the table. In Table 2.1, the left-hand column lists the most likely emotions to be repressed; the second column lists, as noted, the particular defense mechanism; the third column lists the emotion that emerges with transmutation; and the fourth column delineates the potential targets of the transmuted emotion.

Displacement is a very common defense mechanism that "displaces" the negative emotion away from self onto other individuals. Typically, repressed anger is the most common form of displacement; individuals may be angry at themselves and/or another who is too important or powerful to sanction negatively, with the result that the anger is turned on others who are available, too weak to fight back, or not important. This also relates to other emotions, such as guilt or shame, which contain an anger component that then becomes the dominant emotion that is displaced. Moreover, like all defense mechanisms, the emotion can be displaced onto social structures or members of social categories. For instance, an individual who is angry may displace his or her anger toward another, or a social structure like a corporation, or a social category like

Table 2.1 Repression, Defense, Transmutation, and Targeting of Emotions

Repressed emotions	Defense mechanism	Transmutation to	Target of
anger, sadness, fear, shame, and guilt	displacement	anger	others, corporate units, and categoric units
anger, sadness, fear, shame, and guilt	projection	little, but some anger	imputation of anger, sadness, fear, shame or guilt to dispositional states of others
anger, sadness, fear, shame, and guilt	sublimation	positive emotions	tasks in corporate units
anger, sadness, fear, shame, guilt	reaction-formation	positive emotion	others, corporate units, and categoric units
anger, sadness, fear, shame, and guilt	attribution	anger	others, corporate units, or categoric units

a gender or ethnic group. The key to displacement is to change the target of the emotion transmute it to another emotion, and since this emotion does not have to be converted to another "safer" emotion, it is a commonly used defense mechanism because it protects the integrity of self and pushes the emotion onto safer objects. Yet, displaced anger, if directed at another, may invite counter-anger and negative sanctions that can be highly disruptive to social relations. For this reason, individuals often displace their anger onto others who are not in a position to fight back—the dog, children, spouses (if they are too afraid to fight back), members of social categories, or highly remote others (the president, Congress, etc.).

Projection involves taking the emotions felt by self, repressing them, and then attributing these emotions to others. A person who is angry may ask another "Why are you so angry?" Or, a shamed or guilty person may inform the other that he or she should not feel shamed or guilty. If emotions besides anger are projected onto another, there is also a bit of anger or aggression added in. Projection always irritates the other who is "accused" of experiencing and acting out an emotion that is not felt. However, projection can be a self-fulfilling prophecy when anger is involved; people get angry at those who project their anger onto them, and thus, they soon become angry at the person who projected—making them even more frustrated and angry at the other. Once we look for it, projection is a very common defense mechanisms because it does not require transmutation of the emotion but only, like displacement, shifting the locale of the emotion—in the case of projection, imputing the emotion to other(s).

Sublimation involves changing the polarity of a negative emotion from negative to positive, typically in collective enterprises like work. For example, an individual who hates work becomes a positive emotion-generating cheerleader for tasks to be completed. Sublimation protects people from having to experience negative emotions about what they are doing that might rub off on self as a negative person stuck in an unpleasant situation. This kind of flip-flop of emotional polarity is difficult and usually emerges when persons are trapped in a chronically negative situation from which they cannot escape.

Reaction-formation is also a polarity-changing emotion like sublimation but it can be employed to change the emotions not only toward situations but also others, social structures, or categories of persons about which a person has intense negative feelings that harm self. Reaction-formation is often activated when individuals have conflicting emotions toward other(s) like a parent or parents; and after experiencing a collage of negative emotions like anger, shame, or guilt at the hands of another or others, the emotional conflict is denied by over-zealous displays of positive emotions toward the persons or persons who have caused emotional pain. For example, a son who subconsciously hates his father displays and professes great love for this hated object; a person who hates members of an ethnic minority, but must interact with them, is overly friendly toward them; a person who hates his job professes his commitment to the corporation where he or she works.

Attribution is generally not thought of as a defense mechanism, but from a sociological perspective it may be the most important if we are to understand emotions in societies. Hence, a bit more time will be devoted to explaining attribution dynamics in general and how they can also operate as a defense mechanisms.

How Do Attribution Processes Extend the Reach of Negative Emotions?

Gestalt social psychologists (e.g., Heider 1946, 1958) noted long ago that individuals tend to make causal attributions for their experiences. They attempt to discover the source of their behaviors and those of others, and to map the causal connections between situations and the actions of others, on the one side, and their feelings and behaviors on the other. For example, a person feeling anger will try to discover the cause of this anger, and in so doing, this person is making an attribution for the experience. This general cognitive process is basic to humans and can also work as a defense mechanism when individuals are trying to protect self from negative emotions. Individuals will generally seek to make attributions for all emotional experiences, primarily because emotions always make people self-aware. When self is pulled into emotional experience, it automatically becomes an object of evaluation; and when individuals try to avoid negative emotions like *shame, guilt, fear,* or *sadness,* they will often try to make attributions about the source of these and other emotions. As long as this process avoids repression, it can be very healthy for a person to understand who and what social structures have caused pleasant or unpleasant emotional experiences. But, when the negative emotions are repressed, individuals can begin to make more extended attributions, seeing others, categories of others, situations, social structures, and other social objects as responsible for the events that led to negative emotional feelings about self. In this manner, people, categories of people, or social structures are blamed for negative emotions—thereby protecting self. Of course, if a person makes a self-attribution for an emotional response, they will experience emotions such as anger at self, shame, guilt, and other appropriate emotions directed at self. Thus, persons who have experienced shame and blame themselves for this feeling will experience a new round of shame—additional layers of shame for acting in ways that generated shame in the first place. People become, in essence, "ashamed of being ashamed." Yet, there is always a bias for such negative emotions to move away from self; persons generally look outside themselves for the causes of their negative emotions, seeking to find others and social objects to blame for their feelings.

When persons blame others or social objects like categories of others or social structures for their negative emotions about themselves or for negative experiences, they will generally repress a complex emotion like shame, guilt, and first-order elaborations, which in turn leads to intensification and transmutation of these emotions into anger that then targets others, categories of others, and social structures. The anger becomes, in essence, a heat-seeking missile looking for a safe target of attribution. Other complex emotions like alienation also activate attribution processes because persons almost always blame social structures for their sense of disengagement rather than themselves.

There are, in fact, a limited number of objects about which attributions can be made in the social world, and what is true of attributions is also the case for the targets of the transmuted emotions generated by other defense mechanisms. These targets are:

1. Self composed of different types and levels of identity formation (to be discussed shortly).
2. Other(s) in the local situation or at other locations in the division of labor of **corporate units**.
3. Local situation where interaction has occurred.
4. Structure and culture of the corporate unit in which the situation is embedded.
5. **Categoric units**, which define individuals as being marked by distinctive characteristics, as is the case for age, gender, ethnicity, religious affiliation, or virtually any marker of difference that allows people to be put into a category.
6. **Institutional domains** (like economy, polity, religion, medicine, education).
7. **Stratification** systems as a whole (composed of classes ranked by their members' shares of valued resources).
8. Society as a whole.
9. Another society or set of societies.

There are two basic principles of attributions for emotions (Lawler 1992, 1997, 2001; Lawler and Thye 2006; Turner 2007a). One is that positive emotions reveal a **proximal bias**, with individuals making self-attributions or attributions to local others in the situation for their positive emotional experiences. The other is that negative emotions evidence, as I have noted, a **distal bias**, with individuals making attributions to more remote objects outside the local situation—objects like corporate and categoric units, an institutional domain, the stratification system, the society, or even another society. In this way self is protected, and the person does not have to risk counter-anger from those in the local situation who can fight back and make life even more emotionally unpleasant for a person already experiencing negative emotions about self.

Attribution processes dramatically extend the reach of emotional energy experienced by persons. If negative emotions can target more remote social structures and if they can be charged up, then these emotions can have large effects on a society. For example, international terrorists come from countries where they have often experienced shame (for failing to realize their goals in their society), but this shame is often repressed and transmuted to diffuse anger directed at such a remote object as the United States or "the West" more generally. Most of the problems experienced by terrorists are the outcome of political corruption and class stratification in their own societies, but through manipulation of people's emotions by local media and political leaders, the emotions target another society, often with tragic results like 9/11. Historically, Great Britain was more responsible for the current geopolitical and domestic problems in the Middle East than the United States (although the invasion of Iraq dramatically increased the perception that the United States was the problem, a sentiment that is intensified by the United States' support of Israel). Yet, once emotions are repressed, the exact origin of these emotions is often lost; the result is that these emotions become, as noted earlier, heat-seeking missiles needing a guidance system, which can be provided by local terrorist cells, media, and political leaders in the countries where the repressed emotions first arose. Thus, negative emotions that are repressed will become more distal, with the result that they can have large effects on societies.

Moreover, there can be simple direct anger that is not repressed toward a society if this society is perceived to have caused harm and humiliation that will always arouse negative emotions, but the charging up of emotions to the point where people are willing to kill themselves in acts of vengeance is likely to be driven by shame that has been repressed, with the direct anger experienced simply adding to the diffuse anger arising from transmutation of shame. And, the more a foreign society metaphorically "pokes angry people in the eye" with its policies, the more attention it draws to itself, thus becoming an easy target in attribution dynamics.

Another problem built into the proximal bias for positive emotions and distal bias for negative emotions is that positive emotions stay local while negative emotions target the society and its key institutions. But, if positive emotions stay local in encounters and situations of face-to-face interaction, how can they be used to legitimate macrostructures like a society's institutions and stratification systems, or the society as a whole? This is one of many dilemmas posed by human emotions. Legitimization and commitments to macrostructures are essential for a society's viability, but how are the positive emotions that drive legitimization and commitments to break out of the micro-level of interpersonal behavior and move toward macrostructures? This movement of positive emotions more distally is critical because negative emotions *almost always* tend to move outward away from self and local situations, and so unless conditions allow positive emotions to move outward, a disproportionate amount of negative emotional energy will be directed at macrostructures—a sure formula for problems in a society. Thus, these biases—proximal for positive emotions and distal for negative emotions—are critical to understanding the problem of emotions in societies, as we will see in Chapter IV.

Basic Conditions of Emotional Arousal

Emotions are aroused under two basic conditions: (1) meeting or failing to meet expectations in a situation; and (2) receiving positive or negative sanctions (Turner 2007a, 2008, 2010a, 2010b). When people meet expectations and/or receive positive sanctions from others, they experience positive emotions, whereas when they fail to meet expectations and/or receive negative sanctions from others, they experience negative emotions. Virtually all situations reveal normative expectations, but there are many other sources of expectations, including: having one's sense of self verified by others, receiving expected or even unexpected resources, and experiencing positive emotions from pleasant interactions.

There are many more sources of expectations, but the critical point is this: if important expectations that persons brought to a situation are not met, they will experience negative emotions; and as I will emphasize shortly, if their sense of self is not verified, the level of negative emotions aroused will be significantly greater. This simple point can be brought home from your experiences of taking an examination: if you expected to do well, but in the end did not get the grade that you expected on the test, you will experience a potential array of negative emotions—anger, frustration, fear, sadness, and many others. My personal experience is that students make an external attribution and blame me and my test more than themselves, which is perhaps understandable because we all seek to protect self from negative emotions. If, moreover, your identity or future identity was on the line for this test—say, it was in your major and critical to moving onto graduate school—your distress will be that much greater. You may experience shame or guilt, and even repress these emotions, which will emerge as anger at a more distal target. This kind of personal experience occurs constantly in people lives; and when expectations are consistently unmet, people may lower the bar and expect less, but along the way they have experienced and perhaps at times repressed a full palate of negative emotions that will not easily go away. These emotions will drive attributions, mostly external directed toward distal targets. If enough people have such experiences and make these attributions, this collective arousal can be a powder keg of pent-up emotions that can explode on a society—just as if someone set off a big bomb.

Conversely, when people's expectations are realized, they experience positive emotions and give off positive emotions to others around them. And, if individuals consistently experience positive emotions because they have met expectations in a wide variety of situations in many diverse institutional domains (e.g., economy, family, education, religion, sport, arts, and other domains), positive emotions begin to go more distal. People begin to perceive that the larger social structures of society bring positive good and, as a result, they begin to develop commitments to the institutions and even the stratification system, as well as the society as a whole. They see the macro social world as legitimate, with the result that a society will become more stable and less likely to experience disruptions fueled by negative emotions. This simple and perhaps obvious generalization is important to remember because it is one of the fundamental conditions under which positive emotions can break out of the proximal bias and become more distal.

Negative and positive sanctions have these same effects. When individuals chronically experience negative sanctions, they experience many negative emotions; and if people experience potentially deadly emotions like shame or even humiliation from sanctions, then repression, transmutation, and attributions toward not just others but social structures becomes more likely. Moreover, failure to meet expectations is related to negative sanctions as this failure can seem like a sanction or even be conflated with an inability to meet expectations. As a consequence, the intensity of negative emotional energy may double since both sources of negative emotional arousal are activated. Conversely, positive sanctions arouse positive emotions, and the more one's sense of self is on the line, the more positive will be the emotional arousal. And, if individuals consistently receive positive sanctions across a wide variety of situations in many different institutional domains, the positive emotions aroused can begin to go distal, leading people to commit to and legitimize macrostructures and whole societies.

These fundamental conditions of emotional arousal—that is, expectations and sanctioning—can occur in virtually all situations. In fact, they are part of being humans who live in social structures and abide by cultural norms, beliefs, and **values**. Expectations are always in play, and sanctions are always being meted out. When negative emotions are aroused under one or both of these fundamental conditions and when self is highly salient, repression becomes a likely response to negative emotional arousal. Repression operates as a kind of turbo charger on emotions: they are intensified; their origins are obscured; they are transmuted into emotions that protect self; and they are the rocket fuel (to mix metaphors) of external attributions that can have large consequences on the structure and culture of a society. Thus, built into the very nature of humans and social reality is the potential for both positive emotions that bind us to each other and to society or, on the darker side, for negative emotions that can be turbo-charged into collective actions that change or even tear down social structures, cause violence, or lead to the withdrawal of legitimacy and commitment to the key structures of the society and its culture. Structural and cultural forces that set large numbers of people up for failure in meeting expectations or impose upon them consistently negative sanctions in diverse contexts are, in the end, forces that will cause problems in a society, as we will see in Chapter IV.

Identities and Emotional Arousal

Humans and a few other very intelligent mammals (including all of the great apes) can see themselves as an object in their environment. For humans this behavioral and cognitive capacity is elaborated into a sense of self, as I have mentioned repeatedly. This sense of self is organized into a series of **identities** that, I would argue, are organized at different levels, as outlined in Figure 2.1. At the level of *role-identities*, each of us has a sense of how we play roles, and the more we play a particular role—father, mother, student, son, worker, etc.—the more coherent are our cognitions and emotions associated with this role (Turner 2000). And, most importantly, these emotions and cognitions become expectations for how we should play the role and, even more importantly, how others should respond to us as we play a role. The next level of identities is a *group-identity*, by which I mean more than groups. We often identify with virtually any corporate unit revealing a division of labor in pursuit of goals—a wide variety of groups, probably a somewhat smaller set of organizations, and often a community. Anyone who knows a rabid sports fan and who has visited a sports bar knows how extreme identification with a team can be, even though the fan is not even an actual member of the team. But this does not stop the identification, or the view that life's ups and downs go with the winning and losing, and the adornment of the body with totems (hats, sweat shirts, pants, and other items carrying the team's logo and name). Normally, people do not go to this extreme but we all have identities with various corporate units—our school, fraternity or sorority, the place we work (if we like it), our home town, and many other potential "groups" in which we play roles and with which we form an identity. This identity is a set of cognitions and emotions about our place in a group and how we treat and are treated by others. Often, we experience positive or negative emotions on how this group performs *vis-à-vis* other groups, underscoring the extent to which our sense of self is wrapped up in a group-identity. A third level of identity is a *social-identity*, which is built around the various categoric units to which we belong—gender, age, class, ethnicity, religious affiliation, and other categories that make a difference to people and how they are treated. We carry our social-identity around with us, and it affects how we behave before others and how we see and evaluate ourselves. For example, a man and a women have different gender identities, and these determine how they play roles, how they feel about themselves, how they expect others to treat them, and many other potential cognitive-emotive states. And, we care if people honor and verify our social-identity. The final level of self is *core-identity*, which is the accumulated cognitions and emotions that we have about ourselves as persons. This is the most powerful identity, and we work very hard to make sure that people honor and verify this identity because it embodies our core feelings and cognitions about who we are as persons, carrying a sense of how we should be treated in virtually all situations.

As Figure 2.1 attempts to illustrate, these identities become more inclusive from role-identity to group-identity through social-identity and finally to core-identity.

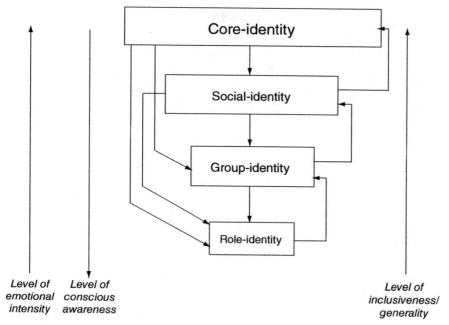

Figure 2.1 Levels of identity formation.

Our social- and core-identities are always with us; our group-identities are with us when we are in the group, although we can also carry this identity into other groups—as a rabid fan does, or as a student will when off campus. The social-identity is hard to escape because other people always categorize others on the basis of visible markers of difference, marking membership in a social category like gender, age, or ethnicity/race. And, of course, our core-identity is always with us, and typically invested in at least some of the roles, groups, and categories that lower-level identities are built around.

Another feature of identities is that we are most conscious of identities at a lower level. You and I can probably describe our behaviors in various role-identities; we can do the same for group-identities, but as we move into social-identities and core-identities, we begin to have trouble describing these higher-order identities. For example, if I asked you how you see yourself as a woman or man, or as a member of an ethnic group, you could say something but your comments would probably sound a bit vague, especially if I also asked you to describe the emotions and feelings tied up in these identities. If I asked you what your conceptions and emotions associated with you as a human being are, you could again say something but it would not be easy to articulate the elements of this identity.

And yet, even though we cannot easily describe these higher-order identities, we have powerful emotions about them. We know immediately when our core-identity or social-identity has been insulted, attacked, or simply not verified by others; the negative emotions being aroused soon tell us that something has gone very wrong. Thus, as

Figure 2.1 documents, as we move from role to core-identity, we lose some capacity to be fully aware (cognitively) of the elements of higher-level identities, whereas the opposite is true of emotions that are immediately aroused when these identities are not verified by others. Our higher-level identities outlined in Figure 2.1 are loaded with emotions, and it does not take very much for those emotions to be aroused.

Emotions become an ever more potentially volatile force when people's identities are not verified or not given the deference that we think we deserve. We will get emotional when our role-identity is not verified, a bit more emotional when our group-identities are not accepted, even more emotional when salient social-identities are not accepted, and dramatically more emotional when our core-identities are not confirmed. We implicitly recognize this fact from our experiences with others, and we almost always—if we can—verify another's identity because we know the consequences if we cannot, or will not, accept the identity that another is presenting: potentially extreme negative emotions that breach the situation and that will take time to bring down. And so, when we think about the problem of emotions—especially the arousal of negative emotions that not only breach local interactions but also have been aroused collectively—the failure of persons to realize expectations for how they should be treated is almost always tied to one, more, or all of the identities that we present to others. And, if social structures and culture persistently operate to prevent people from realizing key identities, negative emotions, and often intense negative emotions, will be constantly aroused. And over time, these emotions, even when repressed, will cause a problem for a society.

Emotions can turn deadly and violent when they arise from a failure to meet expectations of an identity. When people feel that they have not been treated as they should, they experience the full range of negative emotions. And if they experience shame and repress this shame, the transmuted emotion that eventually escapes the cortical sensors will be doubly intense and potentially volatile.

The essence of who we are as humans is, ultimately, tied to the cognitions and emotions marking our various identities; and thus, we all seek to have our identities verified because this is what makes us feel human and generates positive emotions about ourselves. When any identity is not verified, negative emotions are aroused, and when these negative emotions are aroused consistently among larger numbers of people, the more problematic emotions become for the viability of a society. The intensity of the emotional reaction is proportional to the number of times that all levels of identity fail to be verified, although unverified social- or core-identities alone can also cause powerful emotions. What conditions, then, would systematically cause identities to be unverified? One of the most important is stratification, as an emotion- and conflict-generating structure in all complex societies, as we will see in the next chapter.

Summary and Conclusion

Emotions are the essence of well-being, but there is a dark side to emotions that always haunts us as people and, perhaps even more importantly, the societies in which we live. Emotions are aroused under two basic conditions: meeting or failing to meet expectations and receiving positive or negative sanctions. When identities are on the line, and expectations associated with identities are not realized, especially expectations arising from our social- and core-identities, individuals will experience intense emotions. Similarly, when we are negatively sanctioned by others or when we negatively sanction ourselves (in our thoughts about our actions), particularly negative sanctions attacking an identity, persons will, once again, experience intense emotions. Negative emotions are psychologically painful to self and to social relations among persons, and so it should not be surprising that individuals employ various defensive strategies, and when these fail, that they engage in repression of negative emotions about self.

Yet, repressed emotions will almost always reappear, often in more intense and transmuted forms. Repression protects self in the short run, but at a cost to a person's long-term emotional well-being and to each individual's ability to form stable and meaningful social relations. But repression does more; it sets the stage for those emotions that can cause problems for a society—above and beyond the harm done to the person who has repressed negative emotions. Repressed emotions are channeled by secondary defense mechanisms, which affect the valence of the transmuted emotion that will break the cognitive sensors of repression and the target of the emerging emotion. It is this targeting outcome that can have consequences for society when transmuted negative emotions circulate among large numbers of individuals who grow increasingly hostile and violent. Stratification is one of the key structures that can cause negative emotions to accumulate among subpopulations, thereby increasing the potential for mobilization and targeting of key meso and macro social structures in a society—as we will see in Chapter III.

DISCUSSION QUESTIONS

1. Why are emotions repressed and how are identities part of this process?
2. Why are identities so important to humans?
3. Why do humans have multiple identities, with some more inclusive and emotionally balanced than others?
4. Why is attribution an important, perhaps sociologically the most important, defense mechanism?
5. Why are role- and group-identities easier for us to articulate and understand?

III: The Stratification of Emotions

S tratification begins with the unequal distribution of valued resources to people in a society (Turner 1984, 2010a). Over time, social classes are formed on the basis of the relative shares of valued resources that various subpopulations receive; and once classes begin to form, they are ranked by their members' shares of resources. This rank-order is usually highly linear, with distinct upper classes and lower classes, but at times the middle classes are less clearly ranked and often constitute several subpopulations that hold somewhat different types of resources but whose shares of all resources are, on balance, somewhat the same. On the basis of their relative ranks, members of classes are evaluated as more or less worthy, with middle and higher social classes being positively evaluated and with those below the middle suffering increasingly low evaluations, if not outright stigma.

The final element of any stratification system is the rate of mobility of a person or family from one class to another. Rates of mobility depend upon many factors, including the boundaries around classes, prevalence of discrimination against individuals, and opportunities provided by institutional domains.

We can thus define stratification as the unequal distribution of resources, the formation of social classes, the rank-ordering of these classes on a scale of worth, and the rates of mobility of individuals from one class to another. All of these elements of stratification vary, and so societies are, to varying degrees, stratified. It is tempting to view stratification as looking much like layers on a cake, but this image does not completely hold up, except for the upper crust and the bottom layers of this cake; the middle layers, especially in industrial and post-industrial societies, look rather messy, with an absence of straight lines separating layers. Still, even with this mess in the middle, stratification is very real and has large effects on the problem of emotions in society.

Sociologists have, I believe, a rather narrow view of stratification as revolving around the unequal distribution of money, power, and prestige. *Money* is the capacity to buy material wealth and horde many other resources that are valued. Similarly, *power* is the ability to control others and, likewise, to use this control capacity to accumulate other valued resources. *Prestige* is somewhat different because it is the possession of honor, and the right to claim deference from others by virtue of possessing this honor; and at times prestige can be used to garner valued resources, even money and power. Sociologists' emphasis on these resources is a holdover from Karl Marx's and Max Weber's respective analyses of stratification, but in fact many other valued resources are distributed in societies. And so, a fuller consideration of these additional resources changes the dynamics of stratification. Indeed, if we look at the things that people in a society value beyond money, power, and prestige, the unequal distribution of resources becomes more complex and nuanced than the typical formulations of sociologists.

I will argue in this chapter that positive emotions are very much like prestige because they are a highly generalized reinforcer that can be possessed and used in a wide variety of contexts to bring pleasure to individuals. And, like prestige they are unequally distributed and can be used to garner other resources. For a reservoir of positive emotional energy gives people the confidence to secure other resources, just as people's prestige gives them the honor to claim further resources. Some people and families in a society, especially those in the upper and middle classes, have larger shares of positive emotional energy than others, while those in lower social classes hold higher levels of negative emotions than those in middle and upper classes. This unequal distribution of emotions is the outcome of the resources that people hold, and it is for this reason that inequalities in the distribution of positive emotional energy generally correspond to the ranking of social classes (Barbalet 1998).

Yet, some resources are more evenly distributed than others, arousing at least some positive emotions among members of classes below the middle; and this fact often makes inequalities less dramatic than when only money, power, and prestige are considered. In turn, if other resources are less unequally distributed, the same might be true about positive emotions that come from having these resources. Thus, we need to untangle what can be rather complicated patterns of resource distribution, including emotions as an important resource.

The Organization of Societies

To analyze stratification and, at the same time, get a clearer notion of the power of emotions in societies, we need a simple model of how societies are built up. Figure 3.1 offers a conceptual scheme for the basic kinds of structure in human societies at various levels of social organization. Let me start at the top of the figure where macro-level structures are denoted and move down to micro-level structures.

Institutional Domains and Corporate Units

Societies are ultimately constructed from **institutional domains**, which are sets and congeries of corporate or organizational units (see below) that have evolved to meet pressing problems of adaptation of a population to its various environments, including the environments created by complex societies (Turner 2010a). For example, economies emerge because people have to eat and support themselves; and hence, an economy is organized to gather resources, to convert them (through production) into goods and services, and finally, to distribute the outputs of production to members

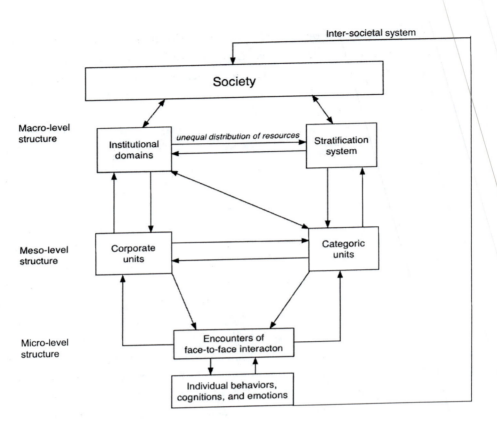

Figure 3.1   A simple conceptual scheme.

of a population in markets using (in more complex societies) money. The same is true for polity or government, if you prefer; it evolves to manage problems of coordination and control of members of a population and the units organizing their activities as well as the need to protect the borders of a society from incursion by other populations; and the greater these problems, the more power will be consolidated and used to regulate and control members of a society and to defend its borders. Kinship was probably the first institution in human societies and it is organized to resolve the problem of reproduction—building safe harbors for infants and children in structures built around marriage of males and females connected by love, loyalty, and affection for each other. All other institutions—law, education, medicine, arts, sport, religion, and the like—evolved to handle other kinds of adaptive problem facing humans and their organization into societies.

Institutions are built from corporate units revealing divisions of labor organized to pursue goals. There are three basic types of corporate units: groups, organizations, and communities. Groups are usually embedded inside organizations, while organizations are located in communities. Resource distributions causing formation of stratification systems come from the unequal distribution of resources by the corporate units in institutional domains. The divisions of labor within the structure of a corporate unit are generally unequal, with those in higher positions in the vertical division of labor receiving more resources than those in lower positions. Moreover, access to some corporate units is often limited, with only some people able to secure resources from corporate units in a given institutional domain. For example, not everyone in the United States has access to corporate units in medicine, in higher education, and in businesses; as a consequence, they cannot receive the valued resources meted out by corporate units in these institutional domains.

Each institutional domain has at least one valued resource that its corporate units distribute unequally. For example, the valued resource of the economy is money; the valued resource of polity or government is power (and authority); the valued resource of kinship and family is love and loyalty; the valued resource of medicine is health; the valued resource of education is learning; the valued resource of religion is sacredness/piety; and so on for all institutional domains. It is not hard to see power and money as resources—because sociologists have emphasized these since the very beginnings of the discipline as the keystones of stratification. But *love* and *loyalty* are also resources, as are *health, sacredness/piety*, and *learning*; and like all resources, they are highly valued by people and distributed unequally.

It may, at first, be difficult to grasp quite how these seeming less tangible resources are the same as money or power, but they are. In reality, money and power are not quite as tangible as we might think. If you hold a five-dollar bill in your hand, it is valuable for what it symbolizes: units of purchasing power. The bill itself is not valuable, as you would immediately see if the ink were wiped off. The same is true with power; it is a symbolic medium by which people are able to tell others what to do. True, sometimes physical coercion occurs and thus power seem very real, but power is often a symbol marking this ability to engage in other means of control, such as giving orders. Love and loyalty in the family are affective states—in the case of love, a real emotion—that are a medium by which family members relate to each other and form bonds; and in so doing, love and loyalty become highly valued, despite their seeming intangible character. The same is true of all of the other resources distributed within institutional domains by their constituent corporate units: they are *media*—indeed *symbolic media*—that signify value and that are used to get things done within the corporate unit. For example, people are paid to get work done, love and loyalty are what allow families to function, learning is what organizes school activity, power and authority are used engage in social control, and so on.

I am trying to resurrect an old idea with this notion of **generalized symbolic media of exchange**, which are the means for discourse, interaction, exchange, and formation of ideologies within institutional domains, while at the same time being the valued resources that are distributed unequally by corporate units. As is evident, generalized symbolic media are complex. In Table 3.1, I have listed and briefly defined the generalized symbolic media that actors in corporate units within each institutional domain utilize.

Table 3.1 Generalized Symbolic Media of Institutional Domains

Economy	**Money** and other metrics of value that can be converted into money
Polity	**Power** or the capacity to control the actions of other actors
Law	**Influence** or the capacity to define what is just and right for actors as well as the ability to adjudicate social relations among actors
Religion	**Sacred/supernatural** or the ability to explain events in terms of the power and influence of non-observable forces
Education	**Transmission** of knowledge or the capacity to impart knowledge to actors
Kinship	**Love/loyalty** or the use of strong affective states to engender strong attachments and commitments among kin
Science	**Verifiable knowledge/truth** or the search for knowledge in the empirical world revealing truths about the operation of this world
Medicine	**Health** or the ability to sustain the normal functioning of the human body
Sports	**Competitiveness**, or socially constructed situations where winners and losers among players are determined and evaluated
Arts	**Aesthetics**, or the commitment to make and evaluate objects and performances by standards of beauty and pleasure that they give observers

As the definition above indicates, generalized symbolic media have fascinating properties. One is that they are exchanged among individuals within a domain—love and loyalty among family members, health for money in medicine, material well-being for money in the economy, power as authority in polity, competition for competition (and today, for money as well) in sport, sacredness/piety in religion (often exchanged for money through donations), aesthetics in art (again, often exchanged for money), verified knowledge in science, learning in education, and so on down the list of institutions. Thus, the generalized symbolic media are the "coinage" of an "institutional realm"; they are what members use in forming exchange relations, although media from other domains, such as money from economy and authority franchised by polity, also circulate in the organizations of many other institutional domains.

The media are also the valued resources that are unequally distributed by corporate units in institutional domains—as I emphasized above. As such, they are the resources that make up a stratification system. All of the media listed in Table 3.1 are valuable, *per se*, but they are also valuable because they enable people to operate within a domain and to have a resource to exchange for other symbolic media from other domains. For example, love/loyalty, or at least the loyalty part of this medium, is exchanged for money by family members who work in the economy; similarly loyalty from family members (and sometimes love among super-patriots) is exchanged for rights to authority from polity and law; money is exchanged for the right to feel part of the competitiveness of sports. What these examples illustrate is that a medium can be given by one person for the same medium in return—for example, love for love in return, learning for learning. But, often one medium is given up for another—for instance loyalty for money and authoritative rights, money for learning. There is, then, a number of different media circulating in most institutional domains—some indigenous to the domain, others from the outside. Thus, a corporate unit in an institutional domain can distribute its own resources and those of other domains. For example, in higher education, one exchange involves paying money or fees in exchange for learning, but there are other media also circulating, such as verified knowledge from science, authority from polity, money from tax-payers, influence from law, and prestige for high-ranking faculty and administrators. To focus on part of this exchange, polity gives money to fund much of the higher education and franchises power as authority (backed up by influence from law) to corporate units to organize the process of learning and creation of verified knowledge; and in exchange for these resources, polity receives educated workers and new knowledge for its own operations but also for the success of other corporate units in other domains that, eventually, pay taxes used to support the operations of government.

There is, then, a lot of action here; symbolic media are the means by which things get done within and between domains. They are exchanged because they symbolize value, and so when learning and money are exchanged, or money and sacredness/piety are exchanged, parties do so because these symbolic media have value, *per se*, and have the capacity to keep the divisions of labor in corporate units—schools and churches, for instance—operating. Depending upon one's place in the division of labor of corporate units within institutional domains, a person will get more or less of these generalized symbolic media as resources. But once we open our eyes a bit as to what the resources being exchanged and circulating in corporate units are, there are more valued resources being distributed than money and power (as authority). These include *sacredness/piety, learning, verified knowledge, health, competitiveness, aesthetics, influence,* and the other symbolic media listed in Table 3.1. And these resources, as they circulate through divisions of labor of corporate units, are also being distributed unequally to individuals and, hence, become part of the stratification system—to be discussed in more detail shortly.

There is another intriguing property of symbolic media. As symbols, they are used to structure talk and discourse among individuals within an institutional domain. Families talk about love and loyalty; educators talk in terms of learning; politicians talk about power, getting and using it; ministers and church-goers talk about sacredness and piety; artists talk about aesthetics; athletes about competition; doctors about health, and so on. Hence, the generalized symbolic media are also the terms of day-to-day discourse, above and beyond their value as resources in exchanges. As people talk, they develop themes and perspectives using these media (Luhmann 1982, 1988). For example, people in capitalist economies talk about making money and from this talk comes themes that become codified into beliefs that accumulating wealth is a good thing; or educators develop themes about how learning should occur and what the best methods for learning are; doctors and medical personnel develop themes for achieving health; and ministers and their flock develop themes about how best to be pious and to communicate with the sacred in the supernatural world; and so it goes for individuals in corporate units in all domains.

As discourse and theme-making occur, yet another property of symbolic media emerges: **ideologies**, which are powerful beliefs specifying what are good, right, and proper behaviors and actions within an institutional domain. Every institutional domain has a general ideology about how learning, money-making, power use, health, aesthetics, knowledge creation, influence over rights, piety and contact with the sacred, love and loyalty, and so on *should* and *ought* to be achieved. Talk, discourse, and theme-making thus become codified into the evaluative tenets of ideologies. And once these ideologies are in place, they work to constrain the options of actors and to direct how they should and ought to use, exchange, and distribute symbolic media. Actions in domains are increasingly legitimated by, and made to seem right and proper by, the ideology of a domain. People evaluate themselves and others in terms of how closely they have adhered to the ideology of a domain, giving praise to those who embrace and embody the ideology and negative sanctions as well as stigma to those who do not.

Ideologies also legitimate inequality in the distribution of the valued resource(s) in an institutional domain, which is the very symbolic material from which the legitimating ideology is built. This conflation of resources and the symbols used to form ideologies legitimating the unequal distribution of resources makes ideologies very powerful. Ideologies make the pattern of resource distribution seem right and proper—even if an outsider would see it as unfair. Thus, as corporate units within institutional domains distribute resources unequally, ideologies begin to emerge to legitimate the way that corporate units operate, including how they distribute valued resources to their incumbents. Emerging from institutional domains, then, are the basic symbolic materials for creating stratification systems—the other macro-level building block of societies.

Stratification Systems and Categoric Units

As noted at the very outset, stratification systems are built from the unequal distribution of resources to members of a population. We now know how this distribution occurs—corporate units within institutional domains—and the resources that are distributed unequally—generalized symbolic media. And, these media are also the symbols from which the ideology legitimating the unequal distribution of each resource is built—giving them extra power because they are so intertwined with the resource that is unequally distributed. Stratification systems vary enormously in how resources are distributed, how homogeneous and discrete classes holding similar shares of resources are, how linear the rank-ordering of classes is, how much worth or stigma members of classes have, how much prestige can be claimed from possession of resources, and how much mobility across classes occurs. In the United States, for example, there is a number of vaguely defined "middle classes" whose members hold somewhat different configurations of resources, and so, who are hard to rank-order. Upper-middle classes and upper classes are more clearly marked, as are lower-working classes and the poor. This pattern is typical of post-industrial societies, but American society is somewhat unique in how big and amorphous the middle classes are, how large its poverty sector is, and how rich top members of the upper classes are. Other societies at various points of development often have much smaller middle classes that are more identifiable, significantly larger lower classes, and an elite class very much divorced from both middle and lower classes.

As a general rule, the more stratified is a society, the more likely is it to evidence tensions; and the more these tensions are the result of not just inequalities in generalized symbolic media but also inequalities in the distribution of positive emotions—a point to which we will return after a bit more preliminary work. When I emphasize the degree of stratification, I mean the degree of inequality of *all* resources, the degree or correlation among recipients of these resources (those receiving high, middle, or low shares of one resource receive high, middle, or low shares of all other resources), the discreteness of class boundaries and homogeneity of people in these classes, the degree of rank-ordering of classes, the relative worth and stigma among those in high, middle, and lower classes, and the power of ideologies to legitimate this system. The more these conditions prevail, the more stratified is a society and, in the long run, the more it will generate tensions fueled by emotions.

In all societies, there are a few dominant institutions. This fact has large consequences for stratification, because the symbolic media of these institutional domains and their respective ideologies will dominate in the society as a whole but also, for our purposes here, the formation of the stratification systems. For example, if economy, polity, and education dominate over other domains, their ideologies will also be disproportionately influential, and the symbolic media distributed by these domains will be the most valued. Or, if religion and polity dominate, their symbolic media will influence ideologies legitimating stratification more than ideologies from other domains, and their resources will be the most valued. What often emerges is a kind of **meta-ideology** that combines the tenets of all institutional ideologies into a composite ideology legitimating the stratification systems. For instance, it could be argued that economy, education, science, polity and law are the dominant institutions in American society, although other institutions are still very important; the result is that the ideologies of these domains disproportionately influence the formation of the meta-ideology that combines the ideologies of all domains. And it is the resources from these more dominant domains that are the most valuable and visibly displayed. Thus, resources of other domains are less valued, at least by the tenets of the meta-ideology.

Because of meta-ideologies, we can gain the impression that these are *the only* resources of value determining the structure of stratification. But, there are other resources from other domains that are highly valuable—resources like *health, love/*

loyalty, sacredness/piety, aesthetics, competition. If people have these, but lack high shares of money, education, and power, sociology's emphasis on money, power, and prestige as *the* stratifying resources will miss an important property of stratification: the lower correlation among other symbolic media as resources compared to the higher correlation between power, money, and prestige. If we look only at power, money, and prestige, we focus on dominant institutions, to be sure, but we miss *the more equal distribution of other symbolic media*. It is not that there is equality in the distribution of these—for instance, *health* is very much correlated with money in the United States. But there is more variability in the distribution of these resources, and this fact has consequences for how volatile a stratification system becomes.

Another feature of stratification is that of memberships' *categoric units* (Blau 1977, 1994). Categoric units are built around a social category that marks differences that affect how people are evaluated and treated in a society. Prominent types of categoric units are based upon ethnicity, religious affiliation, age, gender, sexual preferences, social class, and virtually any differences that people notice and use to put a person in a category that is differentially valued and that leads to differential treatment of persons in a category. When membership of categoric units—say, ethnic or even gender categories—correlates with the distribution of highly valued resources—for instance, money, power, prestige, education—the stratification takes on new dimensions, and often a new volatility. People's social-identities, and often their group-identities as well, are tied up with their memberships in categoric units; and if this membership is devalued and if discrimination keeps these members from securing valued resources, then an additional layer of tension is built into stratification dynamics. For example, if dark-skinned people are discriminated against and not allowed access to corporate units in economy, polity, and education or are only allowed to participate in the lower positions of corporate units in these domains, this correlation between ethnicity and low levels of resource shares raises the tensions in the stratification system. It is one thing to not have much money, power, learning, and prestige that comes from these resources, but when ethnic social-identities and perhaps group-identities from ethnically based corporate units are highly salient and become the basis for active discrimination, this insult to powerful identities doubles the negative emotions of not having money, power, education, or prestige. As I emphasized in the last chapters, people's identities are highly charged with emotions, and to insult, defile, and discriminate on the basis of a social-identity is to invite double trouble: negative emotional arousal over class position, multiplied by the insult to strongly held emotions about self. Thus, ethnic stratification always makes for more tension in a society.

When categoric units at the meso level become correlated with the macro-level properties of the stratification system, the problem of emotions in society can increase. Much of this emotional potential, however, is built up at the micro level of social reality. People's emotional experiences can come from media and other ways of seeing the world vicariously, but the most important source of emotions is what happens in the smallest unit of society: *focused encounters* among individuals in interaction. Thus, before fully exploring the implications of emotional stratification, we need to examine this micro level of society because it is here that emotional energies—whether negative or positive—are generated and charged up.

Encounters and the Arousal of Emotions

A **focused encounter** is an episode of face-to-face interaction among individuals where they focus on each other and a topic; out of such interactions come a rhythmic synchronization of talk and bodies, a "we feeling," and emotional arousal (Collins 1975, 2004; Goffman 1959, 1961, 1967, 1981, 1983). When people fail to meet expectations, or when they receive negative sanctions, negative emotions are aroused; and these emotions are almost always aroused in micro-level face-to-face encounters. All of the negative emotions that are subject to the dynamics of repression, intensification, and transmutation come from encounters generally lodged inside of corporate units and categoric units. At locations in the divisions of labor of corporate units, individuals interact and experience emotions, depending upon whether they have met expectations and received positive sanctions or the converse. The expectations come from people's identities and from the ideologies of the domain in which a corporate unit is embedded, and these expectations also become part of the normative system of a corporate unit. Similarly, all interactions are embedded in categoric units that are often lodged in the macro-level stratifications system. Social class is itself a categoric unit but if memberships in other categoric units, such as ethnicity, religious affiliation, gender, age, and other distinctions that are salient in a society, correlate with class membership, then this compounding of categoric units creates more potential for emotional arousal, and especially so when people interact.

At first it may seem difficult to see an interaction as embedded in a social category, but a moment's reflection can reveal that such is the case. For example, an interaction among a number of males and females is embedded in these two gender-based categoric units because what transpires in this encounter is influenced by status beliefs about males and females. **Status beliefs** are ideas that people hold about the characteristics of individuals in categoric units (Berger 1988; Ridgeway 1982, 1998; Ridgeway and Correll 2004; Ridgeway and Erickson 2000; Ridgeway and Johnson 1990; Ridgeway and Walker 1995; Ridgeway et al. 1998); these beliefs carry evaluations of the moral worth of members in categories and expectations for how they will, and should, behave. Thus, males and females in societies are often differentially evaluated, with clear expectations for how they should behave and interact in encounters. The expectations inherent in status beliefs are generally derived from the tenets of the meta-ideology legitimating the stratification system as a whole. To take another example, an encounter among members of different ethnic subpopulations (each constituting an ethnicity-based categoric unit) will be conducted by the expectations and relative evaluations of each distinct ethnic participant to the encounter—at least initially. If members of more valued categoric units look down upon members of more stigmatized categoric units, then this interaction will reinforce the general structure of the stratification system and the meta-ideology legitimating its form and operation. As this interaction unfolds, emotions are aroused, especially if members of devalued ethnic categoric units are treated as inferiors. Even when individuals are trying to be polite when interacting with their "inferiors" (as determined by status beliefs), they often come off as patronizing and, in this way, assert their superiority over members of inferior social categories.

Thus, the effects of stratification on emotional arousal are influenced by interactions among individuals in differentially evaluated categoric units. Moreover, members of categoric units are often discriminated against in their efforts to gain access to resource-distributing corporate units in institutional domains or they experience discrimination in not being able to be upwardly mobile in those corporate units where they are incumbent; in either case, they will experience negative emotions as a consequence of discrimatory interactions that deny them access to resources and that, at the same time, insult their social-identities.

Repeated and constant experiences of negative emotional arousal by members of categoric units in face-to-face interactions or focused encounters in corporate units can thus generate negative emotions among those who are devalued, even when the interaction appears to flow with polite demeanor. Moreover, there is another class of encounters—often termed *unfocused encounters*—where these same dynamics can occur. An **unfocused encounter** usually occurs in public spaces where people monitor each others' actions and movements in space *without* direct face-engagement (Goffman 1963, 1971), which would immediately focus the encounter and require direct face-to-face interaction. There are often expectations for how members of categoric units are to conduct themselves in public places—for example, rules about how one should talk, where one can move, what places one can enter, where one can sit, and other implicit norms about what options are available to members of devalued categoric units. Segregation of public facilities in the American South during and after the Civil War are good examples of how devalued categoric units must experience their stigma even in public places. To be denied access to a drinking fountain, to a theater or hotel, to churches with white members, to a bench occupied by "superiors" and other such discriminatory norms inevitably rekindles the tensions and emotions inhering in the stratification system, even without direct face-to-face interaction with "superiors."

The important consideration, then, is to what extent inequalities inhering in the stratification system generate inequalities in focused and unfocused encounters at the micro level of social organization. If individuals must endure interactions in which their identities are not verified, their sense of worth is diminished, their access to facilities is questioned, and, more generally, their access to valued resources is systematically denied, then these interactions will arouse negative emotions that, over time, can pose problems for a society. And, if these negative emotions are repressed, intensified, and transmuted into diffuse anger, then the volatility of emotions will rise and the potential for problems at the meso and macro levels of social organization will only increase.

The Stratification of Emotions

Because people react emotionally to expectations and sanctions, they will always respond emotionally to the expectations for shares of resources that they receive in encounters lodged in corporate and categoric units that, in turn, are embedded in a society's institutional domains and stratification system. If they have very low expectations, then they will ironically react less emotionally when they meet these low expectations, although they may still reveal negative emotions like *alienation*, variants of *sadness*, and even *anger* because they know that their share of resources is low. If their expectations, however low or high, are *not* met and if they feel that they have received negative sanctions in encounters in corporate units within institutional domains that prevented them from receiving their expected resources, they will exhibit more intense variants of *anger* and, potentially, variants of *fear* and *sadness* as well. If they experience *shame*, the emotional experience will be even more difficult, especially if identities of any sort have been on the line, but particularly if social- and core-identities are salient. If the shame is repressed, then diffuse anger is likely to emerge.

The converse is true for individuals who meet or exceed expectations or who perceive that they have been positively sanctioned in the many encounters within corporate units distributing resources. They will feel variants of *satisfaction–happiness*, and if they had some *fear* or *anxiety* about meeting expectations and being positively sanctioned, they will feel *pride* in their accomplishment when receiving resources and positive sanctions.

As people experience negative and positive emotions in encounters within resource-distributing corporate units within institutional domains, they begin to accumulate reservoirs of positive and negative emotional energy. If they have consistently experienced shame, anger, fear, frustration, sadness, and other negative emotions from encounters across many different corporate units embedded in a wide range of institutional domains, they will accumulate a large reservoir of negative emotions. And, if identities have been on the line in these encounters within corporate units, their pool of negative emotional energy will be that much larger. If, in contrast, individuals have been able to secure resources and experience positive emotions in diverse corporate units in varied institutional domains, they will increase their positive emotional energy that, in turn, can be used to continue to acquire more resources in the future. And, if their identities have been on the line, which is more likely when people feel that their expectations will be met and that they will receive positive sanctions, their self-confidence will only increase.

Thus, as a general rule, levels of negative and positive emotional energy build up as people experience emotions in encounters, especially those encounters within resource-distributing corporate units in institutional domains. Their respective reserves of emotional energy will, in turn, determine how they interact in almost all situations. More important for our purposes, their levels of positive or negative emotional energy will determine whether or not individuals will develop commitments to the macrostructures and ideologies of a society.

When individuals have consistently experienced positive emotions across a wide range of different institutional domains, their positive emotions will begin to break the proximal bias of positive emotions (which normally stay local at the level of the encounter), allowing individuals to make distal external attributions to institutions and their ideologies and to the stratification system and the meta-ideology legitimating its operation. It should not be surprising, therefore, that individuals in middle classes and up generally buy into the ideologies of domains and the meta-ideology of the stratification system, giving institutions, stratification systems, and the society as a whole (and even inter-societal systems) legitimacy. They will develop commitments to these macrostructures and thereby act in ways that reproduce these structures. It is for this reason that societies with large middle classes and relatively small lower classes will be more stable because positive emotional energy pushes individuals to make commitments and to bestow legitimacy on macrostructures and their cultures.

When individuals consistently experience negative emotions in encounters across many resource-giving institutional domains, their level of negative emotional energy will be high and, given the distal bias of these emotions, will seek distal targets. Individuals will be more likely, under these conditions, to withdraw legitimacy from the institutional domains where they have not met expectations for receiving resources, the stratification system that has locked them out of participation in corporate units that distribute valued resources, the society as a whole, and even the inter-societal system that is perceived to have worked against the receipt of valued resources. And, their commitments to macrostructures and their cultures will be low. When large numbers of individuals—and especially individuals in identifiable subpopulations where social-identities are highly salient—have consistently experienced negative emotional energy, this energy may increasingly revolve around anger. Anger is a "hot" emotion and will often cause individual and collective actors to attack macrostructures. Thus, as the legitimacy of and commitment to macrostructures decline, and as emotional reservoirs are increasingly filled with diffuse anger, emotions become a large problem for a society.

Typically, people's receipt of resources is somewhat mixed; they receive some but not other valued resources; and thus, they experience a mix of positive and negative emotions. And, in industrial democracies, most people receive some valued resources from some institutional domains, even as they meet with failure in other domains. Conflicting emotions can flip from very positive to negative and be involved in varied commitments to institutional domains, stratification systems, and societies. The key to their general level of commitment to macrostructures is the ratio of positive to negative emotional experiences. If individuals receive more valued resources in more domains than where they do not, they are less likely to take collective action against macrostructures, unless their failures were in domains where important identities were on the line and went unverified. Thus, more than a simple ratio between resources received and not received is involved because some resources are more valuable than others to individuals. Yet, when people cannot receive the resources that they expected in a domain, they may adjust their expectations so that these resources become less important than the resources that can be acquired. Still, if a person's negative emotions linger and if expectations are not adjusted downward, this individual will experience persistent negative emotional arousal that will lead to individual actions or the joining of individuals in collective actions against macrostructures.

As is evident, emotional stratification is complex; and people's emotions can lead to varied actions (Barbalet 1998; Turner 2010b). Predictions of what people will do, then, are not easy to make, even when we understand some of the emotional dynamics involved. In the next chapter, I will try to offer some predictions about how emotions become problematic in societies, but for the present, let me emphasize that it is the stratification of emotions that is an important force in making predictions about how people will feel and how they will act. If we can return to the image of stratification as the layers on a cake that mark classes stacked on top of each other, part of each layer is a modal level of emotional energy for persons and corporate units like families that, collectively, can be viewed as a class's share of a very valued resource: positive emotions. Shares of positive emotional energy are relatively high in all middle, upper-middle, and upper classes because their members have been successful in receiving resources and thus in having positive emotional experiences in encounters across many corporate units in varied institutional domains. There are, to be sure, some negative emotions mixed in here, but the positive energy is much greater than the negative. As we move down the layers of the cake, shares of negative emotional energy increase and at some point they exceed shares of positive emotional energy, at least in many societies. The greater are the shares of negative emotional energy in a social class and the larger is this class, the more its members will pose problems for the stability of a society. Even a smaller class will pose threats for a society if its members experience high levels of emotional energy and have resources that they can use to mobilize for conflict.

Even with the somewhat messy demarcation of various "middle classes," the distribution of people across classes determines how much total negative emotional energy exists in a society. If most people are lower class—as has often been the case in human societies—it is likely that there will be a great deal of negative energy available for mobilization. However, other forces intervene. It is ironic that if a society is highly stratified and if individuals have relatively little chance of being mobile, then they adjust their expectations downward and focus on those corporate units like family and religion where they can receive resources. The result is that total level of negative emotional energy in lower classes is reduced; it is still there but not in such great quantities that it can pose a threat to macrostructures. If, however, those with high shares of resources consistently exploit lower-class individuals and deny them dignity and the capacity to verify key identities, then the store of negative energy in these classes will increase and eventually pose a threat to higher classes and to macrostructures. Thus, there is much to consider when assessing the effects of emotional stratification on societies—as will become even more evident in the next chapter.

Rising Expectations and the Stratification of Emotions

Most societies where there is some level of industrialization systematically generate high expectations, because the values and ideologies of these societies hold out not only the hope but also the expectation that it is possible to be upwardly mobile across classes and to realize the moral codes enshrined in values and ideologies. A **value** is a highly general set of emotionally charged beliefs about what is good–bad, right–wrong, and appropriate–inappropriate in the society as a whole. These values are then translated by institutional *ideologies*, using generalized symbolic media of each domain, into sets of moral codes for each domain. Furthermore, **institutional norms**, or those normative systems, regulating both individual and collective actors' behavior within a domain and directing the norms of the divisions of labor in corporate units within a domain, are constrained by values and ideologies. There is, then, a kind of vertical integration of culture in society, with values providing general moral premises, ideologies specifying these premises within a domain, and institutional norms carrying the moral content of values and ideologies down to corporate units and their divisions of labor. Figure 3.2 outlines the nature of this vertical integration of culture.

The integration of moral codes also influences the formation of meta-ideologies that combine institutional ideologies. Meta-ideologies will thus have a tendency to reinforce value premises because they pull tenets of ideologies that, themselves, had been highly constrained by values during their formation through talk, discourse, and theme-making. Meta-ideologies legitimate the stratification system, including the unequal distribution of emotional energy. All together, these moral codes of culture can aggravate emotional stratification by generating rising expectations that life will get better if the tenets of moral codes are followed. And, in what can be termed **achievement cultures** where moral codes mandate that success can only come with hard work by individuals, failure to realize expectations of moral codes is doubly vexing for individuals. They may feel both shame and guilt, thus setting off a powerful set of emotional dynamics. For example, Table 3.2 summarizes the dominant values of American society (Turner and Musick 1985; Williams, Jr. 1970). As is clear, individuals are expected—indeed, are given a moral command—to be active, to achieve, to progress,

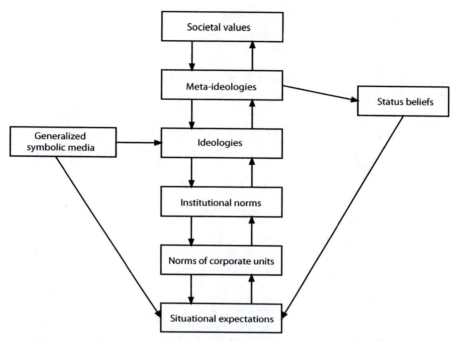

Figure 3.2   The vertical integration of culture.

to master circumstances, and in general to embrace and realize the expectations contained in value premises.

Ideologies, as they translate moral imperatives from values, *systematically* generate
high expectations that cannot always be met because of structural arrangements in
a society that discriminate and/or block access to resource-giving corporate units in
institutional domains (Merton 1938). Once stratification exists, it limits access for
some, often many, to all domains or high positions in their constituent corporate
units, thereby causing many in a society to experience failure in their efforts to meet
expectations and to feel the sting of negative sanctions in encounters within corporate
units when they fail.

A society like the United States thus sets up some people for failure and negative sanctioning, and if there is a systematic bias in failure—that is, members of certain categoric units and class positions are more likely to fail—then the potential for
increasing the store of negative emotional energy increases. And, the failure to realize
these expectations can increase the likelihood of collective mobilization by those with
high reservoirs of negative emotional energy.

Much depends upon the attributions that individuals make. If people blame themselves, then they experience *sadness*, perhaps some *fear* about consequences, and *anger*
(at themselves). They may also experience *shame*, which only increases their sense of
distress. And, they may also feel *guilt* at not having lived up to moral codes. Self-
attributions are painful to individuals but, ironically, promote integration of a society.

Table 3.2 A Brief Overview of Core American Values

Achievement, or the moral mandate that individuals should do well in all situations and should seek to meet criteria in all institutional domains for "success."

Efficiency, or the moral command that individual and corporate actors must not waste time, energy, or resources in order to get things done but, instead, should be rational and prudent in mobilizing their resources to achieve goals.

Activism–mastery, or the moral demand that individuals and corporate actors must seek to master their environments through active efforts to control all contingencies that they encounter and to overcome obstacles that may be present in any environment.

Individualism, or the moral command that the burden to achieve, be active, and master environments falls on the individual more than the collective.

Materialism, or the belief that actors who try to achieve, be efficient, be active, and master their environments are entitled to just material rewards for their efforts and, moreover, that it is a positive good to engage in accumulation of material wealth and that only those who realize these values are entitled to this wealth.

Progress, or the command that actors should always be improving and striving to do better during their life course, and that those who do so are morally superior to those who do not make efforts to improve themselves or their situation in life.

Freedom, or the mandate that actors should be free of constraints by external powers in order to achieve, be active, and progress and that, while all social actors have rights to freedom from undue constraint, the individual has the most right to freedom of all actors in society.

Equality, or the moral belief that individuals should have equalities of opportunity to realize other value premises, but not equality of results unless they have realized other value premises, particularly achievement, activism, materialism, and progress.

Morality, or the view that all matters can and should be judged in moralistic terms as either good or bad, right or wrong and that persons must always seek to determine the absolute goodness, rightness, and appropriateness of their own and others' actions.

Humanitarianism, or the moral commitment to help others who have fallen on hard times that are not their own fault but instead the consequences of circumstances beyond their control.

Conformity, or the moral expectation that individuals will conform to expectations, norms, ideologies, and the value premises of the institutional domains of a society.

Sources: Williams (1970) and Turner and Musick (1985).

When people blame themselves, they are less likely to blame the structure and culture of the society. However, if they repress their negative emotions, especially *shame* and *guilt*, these emotions may transmute into diffuse anger or anxiety. Anxiety is unpleasant for persons, but it does not generally cause them to attack society. In contrast, if shame transmutes into diffuse anger (even after initial self-attributions that blame self), then attributions fueled by *diffuse anger* are more likely to become external and to target social structures and their cultures.

Thus, this combination of achievement values built into American culture and inequalities inhering in stratification will inevitably generate failures for some in meeting expectations and expose them to negative sanctions in resource-giving corporate units in institutional domains. As I emphasized in the last chapter, these dynamics not only cause the stratification of emotions, they also increase the likelihood that individuals will experience negative emotions *collectively*, which makes them more likely to mobilize collectively. For example, when certain categories of persons—ethnic minorities, women, lower-class members, to name the most important categories—cannot realize the success and achievement values of American culture, the negative emotional energy will distribute itself across these categories—thus giving ethnic minorities, women, and lower-class people something in common. And, at a minimum, if social-identities (tied to categoric-unit membership) and in all likelihood core identities, and even group-identities, or role-identities were on the line when people tried to meet culturally generated expectations but were stopped by a combination of discrimination and lack of opportunities in resource-giving corporate units, new layers of negative emotions are added.

Failure to realize moral codes will inevitably invoke **standards of justice**, or ideologies that emphasize that an individual's rewards should be proportionate to their costs and efforts to receive these rewards relative to the costs and efforts of others. Once a sense of justice is activated and used to evaluate outcomes, the emotions involved become *moral*—as responses to standards of what is right, fair, wrong, and unfair. As emotions become moral, they also become more powerful because they invoke people's beliefs about what is fair and unfair, often propelling them to strike out at those perceived to have been unjust—thereby adding to the volatility of negative emotional energy.

If the negative energy is over-represented in social categories—such as those based on class, ethnicity, and gender—then it easier for the individuals in these categories to see common plights and to organize collectively to do something to change social structures. And, when negative emotions emerging from repressed shame by members of categoric units becomes conflated with standards of justice, the emotions become ever more likely to push individuals into collective action.

Conclusion

Societies are built from focused and unfocused encounters, corporate and categoric units, institutions, and stratification systems. Inter-societal systems connecting societies are generally linked via key institutional domains, such as economy, polity, education, and religion whose corporate units establish linkages between two or more societies. All institutional domains generate a generalized symbolic medium that, at one and the same time, is the basis for talk, discourse, theme-building, ideological formation, interaction, and exchange. Actions within a domain involve the exchange of its medium and often media from other domains, such as *money*, franchised *power* as authority, *sacredness/piety* (in theocracies), *learning*, or *verified knowledge*. Interactions of actors in different domains almost always involve at least the exchange of the respective media of each domain, and often more media if these media are in wide circulation.

The valued resources that make up a stratification system are the generalized symbolic media of institutional domains, which, in turn, are legitimated by ideologies built from these same media. The more resources that individuals receive in encounters in corporate units across a range of institutional domains, the more positive will be their emotional reactions and the greater the store of positive emotional energy in their social class. Conversely, the fewer resources that individuals receive in encounters across institutional domains, the greater will be their negative emotional energy; and, if others in their class of origin or in other categoric unit memberships that are correlated with class have similar emotional experiences, the share of negative emotional energy will be high. Emotional energy thus becomes stratified like any other valued resource—whether money, power, prestige, or a generalized symbolic medium that is distributed unequally in a society.

When there are large pools of negative emotional energy in large classes or in categoric units with many members, the potential for tension, conflict, and change increases as individuals withdraw commitment to macrostructures. The potential for individual and collective actions that become problematic for a society depends upon many factors, such as a) the ratio of positive to negative energy, b) the levels of expectations of individuals for valued resources, c) the degree to which individuals adjust expectations downward when they cannot meet initial expectations, d) the extent to which identities are tied up with receiving certain resources, e) the capacity of those resources that are received to compensate for those that are not, and f) the degree to which cultural moral codes raise expectations and lead persons to invoke standards of justice.

DISCUSSION QUESTIONS

1. What is stratification and how is it generated?
2. Why can emotions be considered a stratifying resource?
3. What conditions increase or decrease positive emotions?
4. How do emotions get stratified?
5. How does the stratification of emotions promote stability or change in societies?

IV: The Effects of Emotions on People and Societies

~~~×~~~

Positive emotions make individuals satisfied, if not happy, and more likely to treat others well and to develop commitments to social structures and their cultures. In contrast, negative emotions can pose a problem for society and, as we will see, negative emotions mixed with positive emotions often make for a deadly and explosive cocktail. To get a handle on emotions and society, let me begin with what, for a better term, I will label the *behavioral pathologies* of individuals and, then, successively move into negative emotional arousal that increasingly affects societies and even inter-societal systems.

The label "pathological" is problematic. Indeed, it is often tempting to see the arousal of all negative emotions as "pathological" but we must remember that the human brain is wired to be more emotional than other mammals and that the primary emotional base from which all human emotions are constructed is overwhelmingly negative. Thus, it is somewhat of a miracle that an animal that must use emotions to forge social bonds and develop commitments to ever-more macro societies has been able to stay organized at all. From the perspective of what integrates a society, negative emotions might seem pathological but they are also inevitable. Hence, the key to understanding emotions and society is not so much the arousal of negative emotions *per se*, but the intensity of negative emotions, the number of individuals who consistently experience negative emotions, the accumulated reservoir of negative emotions among members of social classes and other categoric units, and most importantly, how emotions come to be controlled in a society. High levels of emotional stratification, with large numbers of individuals experiencing negative emotions in lower classes and categoric units over-represented in these classes will eventually pose integrative problems for a society.

Personal Behavioral Pathologies

Many people in societies are not emotionally well; they suffer mild to severe emotional strains that make their behaviors dysfunctional for themselves and those around them. Such persons can make local social systems problematic, and even more so if a mentally disturbed person is put in a position of power. But, most of the time, these individuals represent personal tragedies that do not threaten the social order. At times, those who are considered "emotionally disturbed" have been neurologically wired or cross-wired at birth, even if the onset of mental illness takes years if not decades to become manifest. Still, people's experiences in the social world have large effects on how the brain becomes wired and how it operates; and so, there is often a significant sociological aspect to mental illness.

Individuals who have experienced negative emotions during their life course can become mentally ill to the point of no longer being able to function in most normal social situations, or if they do function, they often disrupt social relations, thereby causing others pain and difficulty. The two basic conditions that arouse negative emotions—failures to meet expectations and receipt of negative sanctions—are usually at the core of their difficulties. Important others, such as parents, siblings, friends, and relatives, have meted out negative sanctions or imposed restrictions on meeting expectations, or both. Moreover, such persons have biographies of negative sanctions and failures to meet expectations in the corporate units of key institutional domains, such as family, education, sport, economy, religion, or any domain that has been important to them. And the more a person's identities have been on the line when receiving negative sanctions or failing to meet goals, the more negative will be the emotions experienced or, as is often the case with such painful emotions as shame, the more likely will the emotions be repressed from consciousness (in an effort to protect self). And, the more volatile will the emotions be when they break through the cortical sensors that drive repression. Thus, repression only makes the most painful emotions bearable to a person, but it also increases the potential for severe behavioral pathologies.

Persons who have had to suffer these indignities chronically will have, at the very least, experienced constant *shaming*—the most powerful of the negative emotions that an individual can feel. If these persons have evaluated situations morally, they will have also experienced *guilt* at having failed to measure up to moral codes. If a person can remain conscious of his or her emotional experiences and make accurate attributions for their causes, then this person is more likely to be able to come to terms with negative emotional experiences. For instance, a person may hate their father or mother, feel badly and unfairly treated by teachers or others with institutional power, and if these perceptions are accurate, the individual can act on them. If they are filled with *anger* and *humiliated fury* (extreme shame, mixed with extra doses of anger), they make strike out in violent ways, as can be seen when high school students in the United States and elsewhere use weapons to seek revenge on classmates and teachers. Or, they may become alienated and withdraw, whether by dropping out or dropping drugs, or some other retreatist behavior. These responses make the person dysfunctional in social relations, at least in certain contexts, but they are natural responses to negative experiences that have not been repressed.

More serious pathologies emerge when people have repressed some of their shame and guilt because now the emotions experienced will become more intense and, depending upon the attributions, will morph into one of the three constituent emotions of shame and guilt—that is, anger, fear, or sadness. If repression of shame leads to sadness or clinical depression and fear or anxiety disorders, these emotions are less disruptive to social relations than if diffuse anger becomes the dominant emotion that is felt and released. If repressed guilt leads to anxiety disorders (fear) or to clinical depression (sadness), again the emotions are less harmful to social relations. Of course, all of these negative emotions make the person miserable, often suicidal, but when only the fear and sadness components of shame and guilt come out from the intensification and transmutation process inherent in repression, these emotions certainly disrupt a person's social relations and make life difficult. Still, they do not threaten society or even smaller portions of societies.

Yet anger can turn personal behavioral pathologies into something potentially more deadly for society, especially if larger numbers of individuals have experienced and repressed shame (and at times guilt as well), only to have it emerge as collective *diffuse anger*. When anger leads to individuals to act violently, acts of individual violence will eventually be managed by the forces of social control in a society. When, however, diffuse anger is shared collectively and motivates collective behavior into a change-oriented corporate unit, this anger becomes more dangerous.

Collective Anger and Dangers to Societies

When many individuals in a society have experienced shame and guilt, and have done so collectively and, moreover, have been able to communicate with each other about their experiences, they will often act collectively to alter social structures and their cultures. Furthermore, when there are large numbers of such persons, they provide the impetus to more violent and aggressive actions that can threaten and change the social order of a society and, potentially, system of societies. The key ingredients necessary for such aggressive collective action are (a) the arousal of intense anger, (b) the targeting of this anger through attributions that blame meso and macrostructures and their cultures, (c) the targeting of these structures by organization into corporate units, and (d) the failure of formal mechanisms of social control to repress these aggressive actions.

These ingredients are more likely to be present in highly stratified societies, particularly when the distribution of negative emotional energy is highly unequal. When members of lower social classes and devalued categoric units have large reserves of negative emotional energy, the potential for violence increases. In more democratic societies, where protest can have some effect on the distribution of resources, collective action is more likely to take the form of a social movement organization (McCarthy and Zald 1977), thereby decreasing the chances of extreme violence.

Sometimes, these anger-driven collective actions generated by stratification benefit a society, as was the case with the Civil Rights movement in the United States that dramatically reduced discrimination and inequality on the grounds of ethnicity—thus releasing tensions in a society. At other times, these actions tear apart a society, causing the society to collapse or to be so weakened as to invite conquest by another society. Thus, there are many manifestations of collective anger—some that ultimately reduce tensions, others that increase them to the point of social disintegration. How, then, do we explain these different outcomes? Let me offer one line of explanation.

The Sources of Anger

When individuals have had high expectations for success in institutional domains, but have not achieved that success, they are likely to experience shame and guilt if they viewed their success in moral terms. At the same time, failure to achieve success goals can be seen as a negative sanction, thus increasing the negative emotional arousal. And, during a person's life course, they will have been negatively sanctioned by many others—thus increasing the level of negative emotional arousal. These outcomes are most likely to occur when there is a high level of emotional stratification, coupled with value premises (see Table 3.2) and meta-ideologies emphasizing success, which valorize those who can achieve, while stigmatizing those who are not able to realize success goals contained in moral codes, thereby further increasing the sense of deprivation and, for many, the level of anger.

If individuals do not repress their shame or guilt, they will often make self-attributions—viewing their problems as the result of their own actions. Self-attributions can cause new emotions to emerge from shame and guilt, such as sadness and depression or even anxiety, but when individuals are the target of attribution, shame, and guilt are more likely to lead to behavioral pathologies rather than collective mobilization. And, even if individuals make external attributions to other persons, such as a mother, father, teacher, or employer, the anger may be expressed individually rather than collectively. If, however, the configuration of shame-inducing experiences is much the same among sets of individuals, particularly members of categoric units, then high rates of interaction among similarly shamed persons will increase the potential for mobilization against targets that are perceived (often accurately) to be responsible for the arousal of negative emotions.

There is also another cycle in these dynamics that increases the potential anger driving violence. Individuals often feel "ashamed of being ashamed," thus doubling up the sense of humiliation that can fuel violence. This ashamed-of-being-ashamed cycle can operate subconsciously, or individuals can be cognitively aware of what is happening to them. The likely outcome, in all cases, is that individuals will find targets to vent the shame that has been transmuted into anger that in turn fuels violence (Beck 1999; Lindner 2006; Scheff 1994; Volkan 1997).

The activation of defense mechanisms, particularly repression and attribution, intensifies these dynamics dramatically. Repression denies the emotion—at least for a time—but the energy behind the emotion will eventually resurface in frequently more intensified and almost always in transmuted forms, often as *diffuse anger*. The anger is diffuse because it is always present and, equally important, the source of the anger may be obscured. Indeed, other defense mechanisms may have also kicked in and made accurate attributions difficult (see Table 2.1 for a list of secondary defense mechanisms). Indeed, great love or positive emotions toward the actual source of repressed negative emotions like hatred, fear, and humiliated fury will make the source even more obscure. When the operation of defense mechanisms causes the source of anger to be lost, the anger will reveal a distal bias and move outward beyond self, even beyond others and situations, to ever more meso-level or macro-level targets.

As I stressed in earlier chapters, breaking the connection with the source of the emotion generates a "heat-seeking emotional missile" without a guidance system. It is this kind of free-floating emotional arousal that can, of course, generate personal aggression and violence against anyone or any thing, but the emotions can also be channeled collectively, under conditions to be examined below. We all know people (or, at least, I do) who fly off the handle, who take things too seriously and perceive insults where none are intended, who bully, who get into fights or unnecessary arguments, and who do other aggressive things. It is very likely that these persons have repressed highly painful episodes of shame and failure, only to be stuck in cycles of anger—shame over their anger—more anger. These are also the people who can be mobilized into conceived actions that can indeed threaten the social order.

Attributions

Once emotions are repressed, then, they become more free-floating, but individuals are still likely to make attributions for their feelings and experiences. Attribution is the way that the human brain is cognitively wired. If the emotions are painful to self, then self-attributions become less likely. Moreover, immediate others are often not a good target for venting emotions because they can often fight back and counter-sanction a person. If, however, immediate others cannot fight back, they can then be blamed for another's negative feelings. For example, a good proportion of domestic violence occurs when one person reveals diffuse anger (often the result of repressed shame) and abuses a spouse or children, who cannot fight back. Thus, attributions can stay local if the consequences of aggression, such as physical abuse, can be hidden from others and from agents of social control in a society. As awful as such situations are for those abused, and even for the abuser (who is often racked with shame for his or her aggression), they do not threaten the social order in general, only the micro-level situation in which abuse occurs.

Yet, there are always consequences of venting anger in local encounters and groups because they disrupt relations and often invite negative sanctions in return—which only stokes the underlying shame that caused the anger in the first place. Safer targets are members of categoric units, such as Jews, women, effete intellectuals, liberals, rich, poor, conservatives, and other categories of persons. Here a person develops deep prejudices and then blames members of a categoric unit, typically behind their backs where it is safe. As we will see, when people do so collectively and target the same categories, this kind of venting of diffuse anger can lead to horrific violence. Besides targeting categoric units, corporate units can also become targets as long as one is careful about directly and openly targeting those with power in the division of labor in the corporate unit. Even safer targets are more remote, macro-level structures and their cultures. One can blame the government, as many conservatives do for almost every problem in American society, or one can hate religion, capitalism, socialism, education, or any institutional domain. One can hate injustices generated by the stratification system as a proxy for the repressed injustices to self. Or, as many terrorists do, people can blame another society or culture for their problems (typically generated by shame experiences within their own society).

These kinds of external attributions can persist for a long time and, indeed, they are often passed down across generations—frequently numbering into centuries of external attributions, especially in ethnic communities that sustain beliefs about the evils of categories of others who are responsible for their problems. Equally important, these external attributions fueled by repressed shame can become the motivation for individuals to become organized in ways that lead to extreme violence.

Mixing of Positive and Negative Emotional Energies

When individuals share similar negative emotions and make the same external attributions as to who or what is responsible, they ironically develop positive emotional experiences in talking about external enemies. When such individuals share their grievances in longer-term local encounters within communities, they generally develop common beliefs and world views that can become codified into attributions about the "evil" qualities of others who have done them wrong, now in the present, in the recent past, or even in the distant past. What often occurs is that people who have had similar experiences within institutional domains are members of an ethnic subpopulation or some other categoric unit and/or are likely to live in the same communities, go to the same stores, schools, churches, parks, and other public areas. The result is that they will interact and often inter-marry, thereby creating dense social networks within which the positive emotions associated with sociality circulate. Often, this positive emotional energy is built up by portraying other categoric units (religious or ethnic, for example) or even members of another society (say, Israel or the United States) in highly negative terms. Indeed, local symbols and positive emotions take on focus by developing external targets for the negative emotions that individuals in a community often feel. They thus charge up the positive emotional energy in local encounters (Collins 2008), while externalizing their accumulated negative emotions.

This mixture of positive emotions to charge up negative emotions directed at distal targets is a deadly mixture. Talking about the evils of others or of macrostructures, planning to inflict harm, and eventually seeking to organize for this purpose all increase positive emotional arousal. When local solidarities are sustained by focus on external enemies and ritualized talk and actions to seek revenge on these enemies, now or in the future, the potential for collective violence increases dramatically. The external attributions do not have to be accurate; indeed, they are often considerably off the mark or at least not completely on target. All that is necessary is the maintenance of a culture where beliefs about an "enemy" are sustained, coupled with interactions that charge up reserves of positive emotional energy. Indeed, the flow of positive emotions often depends upon external attributions that push negative emotions toward remote targets.

The Organization of Emotional Energy

For this mix of positive and negative emotions to occur, there must be an incipient or, even better, a more stable set of corporate units within which emotions are aroused. The nature of these groups can vary enormously, ranging from members of an ethnic community who live together or worship in the same place to workers experiencing similar negative emotions at their place of employment onto lower-class street gangs or middle-class terrorist cells. The key ingredients of these structures is that they attract individuals with similar backgrounds, and organize chains of encounters where positive emotional energy is generated by sustaining a focus on enemies (Collins 2008; Turner 2007c).

Other conditions only accelerate these dynamics. One is a leadership structure that can articulate grievances and help codify symbols that facilitate the targeting of negative emotions. Another is media within and between societies that persistently portray targeted societies, subpopulations, or categoric units in negative terms, often deflecting blame from the actual sources of people's negative experiences. For example, one could say that Israel and the United States are hardly to blame for the anger that Saudis often feel and express, but these two countries become targets because of the constant media portrayal of them as enemies of Islam. The plight of the Palestinians is certainly related to the formation of Israel and perhaps the United States' (belated) support of Israel, but it is also the result of the lack of real efforts by other Arab nations to help the Palestinians before and after the formation of Israel. Indeed, it is easier to demonize the West rather than leaders in Arab societies, and in so doing attention is deflected from the real sources of people's problems in various societies in the Middle East. There is, of course, plenty of blame to go around in the problems of individuals and families in the Middle East—only aggravated by the United States' invasion of Iraq—and so the channeling of blame by leaders, politicians, religious spokespersons, and media selectively culls out targets from the many that are actually to blame for the current situation of subpopulations like the Palestinians.

Thus, once people have felt humiliated by their failures to meet expectations, or even suffered the blunt sanction of a soldier's boot or the indifference and corruption of a local official, the shame that is experienced will push people to make an attribution. If all or some of the shame is repressed, then leaders and media can have a much greater effect in moving the attributions to distal targets of their choosing, thus creating the potential for what we see today: international terrorism.

Resources and Mobilization

There is now a rather substantial literature on resource mobilization (e.g., McCarthy and Zald 1977; McCarthy and Zald 2001). Most approaches emphasize organizational, symbolic, financial, leadership, and in a few cases emotional resources necessary to pursue conflict. Conflict can be individualistic, as when one person assaults or kills another, but conflicts that change societies are collective. To organize takes, first of all, organization composed of leaders, an administrative structure, and subunits charged with key tasks, including the implementation of violence. Organization is more effective when there are shared symbols and ideologies that moralize the goals of the organization and, if the organization is focusing on an enemy, that demonize this enemy. Money is critical to support not only the administrative structure of an organization but also its members "in the field," whether a quasi-army or terrorist cell. And finally, the deadly mix of positive and negative emotions should be motivating individuals, increasing their commitments to ideologies, making them more willing to follow leaders, prompting others to provide financial support, and mobilizing sufficient individuals to pursue conflict against an enemy that is seen to have caused negative emotions, despite the potential dangers and costs of conflict.

There is often a gender dynamic in these processes. In most cultures, it is more acceptable for men to reveal anger than it is for women, and in many societies, such as the United States, exhibiting emotions like fear and shame is negatively sanctioned as being "unmanly." Thus, men more than women are likely in a majority of cultures to repress shame, thereby setting up the deadly mix of intensified and transmuted shame into diffuse anger, mixed with positive emotional arousal and group solidarity for venting this anger on chosen enemies (Beck 1999; Volkan 1988). Yet, as is evident when women blow themselves up in acts of terrorism, this gender bias is not universal.

Illustrations of the Power of Emotions and Collective Actions

The above-listed forces in play combine in many different ways to generate collective actions that often pose problems for human societies. As I have emphasized, these problems are all much more likely to become a problem for a society when there is a high level of inequality in the distribution of resources, especially positive and negative emotional energy.

Feuds

In many societies, feuds develop and lock generations of individuals into violent behaviors. Family feuds are common and some become so intense that they sustain violence across generations, as was the case for the famous Hatfield and McCoy feud in the American South. Feuds similar to this are often found in the lore and history of most societies. In more traditional pre-literate societies, such as horticultural populations of the past, a feud-like pattern to war was often evident, with the killing of one person in a tribe by members of another tribe, whether in overt conflict or in ambushes, requiring that this death be avenged, which, in turn, required a vengeful response from the other tribe in a cycle that went on for generations. Thus, while these are not mass killings, they are collectively organized, with each group feeling anger and oftentimes shame or humiliation that others have killed a member of their group, leading them to experience solidarity-generating positive emotions toward their group as they plan revenge on the enemy.

This basic dynamic of "an eye for an eye" is as old as human societies; and it is driven by many of the processes that I have outlined. The shame and anger may remain conscious (Beck 1999), but there may also be repression because collective shame is no easier to deal with than individual shame. And once some of the emotions associated with the loss of a group member at the hands of another group go out of conscious reflection, the level of anger at the enemy will intensify and perhaps become *righteous anger* with a need for *vengeance*. People will feel an extra dose of anger, and they will experience highly positive emotions in planning revenge, in defining the need for revenge in moral terms, and then in executing their righteous anger in violence against others or social structures. (For more examples of these processes, see Scheff 1994; Scheff and Retzinger 1991.) Thus, the solidarity of a group or even a small-scale society is sustained by the feud-like pattern of conflict. Similar dynamics operate for subgroups in societies, such as gangs and ethnic populations.

Gang Violence

Street gangs are a prominent phenomenon in most American cities, and elsewhere in the urban world. These gangs often deal in drugs at the high-risk end of the distribution chain, and they also work to protect "their turf" again incursions by other gangs, not only for control of the local drug market but also for their own sense of group-identity. The result, as we all know, is violence—drive-by shootings (often of innocent, non-gang members), confrontations with police, and actual shoot-outs at clubs, parties, and other more public venues.

If we look at the biography of gang members, it would appear that the general theory of emotions that I (and others) have proposed applies. Gang members will often have had a difficult home life, with at least one and perhaps both parents absent or unstable (perhaps from drug use). Gang members have dropped out of school. And, they are not employable in the normal economy, even as low-wage workers. They have, then, endured failure within key institutional domains and probably received highly negative sanctions from parent(s), teachers, employers, and perhaps even ministers along the way on the road to gang membership. It is very likely, I believe, that many gang members have repressed the shame associated with failures in mainstream institutional domains, generating a sense of diffuse anger that tends to target rival gang members rather than the domains and corporate units in these domains where the shame was originally generated. Gangs rarely attack their own families, schools, former places of employment, or churches; their violence targets other gangs and at times the police.

This pattern documents how repression breaks the connection between the source of negative emotional experiences and the attributions that point the blame at others or social structures. Gang members do not blame self or others in those corporate units where they have failed to meet conventional expectations and where they surely have experienced negative sanctions. The anger is directed at targets that are perceived as "enemies" in what becomes almost a symbolic form of warfare and violence—"an eye for an eye" cycle of violence between two gangs. Their negative emotions toward each other become part of the dynamics arousing positive emotions among each gang's members. The interaction behavior among gang members is highly ritualized with stereotypical greetings and forms of talk, and as they "hang out," their talk and body language falls into synchronization, causing the arousal of positive emotional energy and the development of symbols marking the group vis-à-vis other gangs and groups in their environment (Collins 2004). Much of the talk and discourse among individuals is about the gang, and its symbolization in totems (forms of dress, for example); and these patterns of talk also focus on "enemies," which, in turn, charges up the symbols marking group solidarity. Moreover, as their role-identity, social-identity, group-identity, and even core-identity intersect with the rituals of gang-member interaction and are verified by this interaction, even more positive emotion is charged up. And, with identities now on the line in external conflict with other gangs, it becomes very difficult to stop inter-gang violence.

This mixture of positive emotions among gang members, coupled with the negative "demonization" of rival gangs and perhaps also the police, produces that deadly mixture of positive emotional energy at the proximal level that gives each gang member a source of positive sanctioning, a sense of group-identity, and a perception of accomplishment (as opposed to shame), juxtaposed to the negative emotions (from a lifetime of accumulated shame in the mainstream of society) that are directed outward toward rival gangs. Talk and planning of violence become a key source of positive sanctioning, identity formation, and a sense that expectations are being realized, thus increasing the circulation of positive emotions among gang members. When people's role-, group-, social- and, perhaps, core-identities can only be verified in gangs, when their sources of positive sanctioning come from gangs, when their feelings of efficacy in meeting expectations are only possible in gangs, and when their emotional energy is tied up in the gang's targeting enemies, extreme violence is often the outcome. Violence becomes moralized as sustaining the integrity of the gang and its symbols because these are what allow members to experience positive sanctions and to meet (new sets of) expectations—thereby allowing them to experience pride and other positive emotions and to verify key identities.

Can gangs bring down a society? Probably not in a large society like the United States, but gangs can disintegrate local communities or at least parts of communities, causing people to flee if they can or to barricade themselves in their houses if they cannot escape. The number of gang members in a society like the United States with a population of almost 320 million people is rather small, indeed tiny in a numerical sense, but we can see how much havoc gangs can bring to a community, whether very large cities or smaller communities. There is, then, real potential for larger-scale disintegration built into the emotional dynamics that drive gang formation and actions. In fact, in many societies, gang-like patterns of violence are only a prelude to larger mobilizations that can cause societal disintegration.

Genocide

Why would members of one ethnic subpopulation seek to exterminate those of another subpopulation? Sadly, this kind of collective action has been all too common throughout the world, including the United States during its "Indian Wars." Sometimes the genocide has been indirect, as has been the case when the diseases of one population infect another that has no acquired immunity, as was the case for all of the Americas when Europeans landed, and as was certainly the case when they landed in North America. Indeed, when formerly isolated societies go to war, their germs are often a more powerful weapons than their armaments or armies.

However, I am not addressing this kind of "inadvertent" genocide but instead deliberate efforts to kill categories of people through violent actions. In more recent times, evidence of this form of collective violence can be found in Nazi Germany's killing of at least six million Jews; in central Africa during the 1990s (and even today in Uganda) where centuries of tension between Tutsi and Hutu subpopulations has periodically erupted into mass murders by both ethnic subpopulations; in the break-up of what was once Yugoslavia, where old tensions among religious and ethnic subpopulations led to efforts at extermination before the Western powers intervened; in Northern Ireland where Protestant and Catholics sought to kill one another for much of the 20th century; and so it goes across the globe. Some of these were truly horrific efforts at genocide, and others were confined to violent ethnic conflict that, if one side had gained sufficient power, genocide would have become a real possibility. So, the interesting (but macabre) question is: Why are humans willing to kill their own kind? Relatively few mammals have this propensity and none have it on a mass scale, and thus, why do humans persistently engage in this kind of action?

Again, part of the answer resides in humans' emotionality. Vamik Volkan (2004), a psychiatrist, has written extensively on violence and especially violence revolving around genocide. Earlier, he had posited a "need for enemies" (Volkan 1988), but in more recent work he recognizes that shame is also involved in genocidal violence. His theory emphasizes "the chosen trauma" where one subpopulation has been abused by another, perhaps long in the past. For instance, the defeat of the Serbs by the Turks in the battle of Kosovo in 1396—clearly a long time ago—was the emotional fuel behind the battle cry for ethnic cleansing in the 1990s, after the break-up of the old Yugoslavia. The defeat by Moslems had occurred over 600 years earlier, and in fact, the descendents of the protagonists of 1396 seemed to be living peacefully in Yugoslavia. But once the police-state that was Yugoslavia disappeared, old hatreds that had been passed down for generations surfaced with surprising speed and violence. For Volkan, the key process was the "failure to mourn" losses centuries earlier; and this failure inevitably involved some repression of the shame and humiliation of Serbs at the hands of the Turks, creating diffuse anger that became part of the lore of each Serb family and many of the corporate units in institutional domains organizing Serb activities. There is a shame in the defeat, compounded by shame of being shamed, that eventually leads to some repression of the full sense of shame, but like all emotions that are repressed, they eventually must surface, even shame generated 600 years earlier but passed down in talk and codified into beliefs and righteous anger across generations.

A similar dynamic occurred between the Hutu and Tutsis in Rwanda and Burundi, and sadly appears to have re-emerged in Uganda in 2010. The conflict between these two subpopulations was not wholly along ethnic lines, especially in the genocide in Rwanda, but the basic emotional fuel was the feeling by Hutus that they had been humiliated by the Tutsis, who had gained power and privilege even when they were the ethnic minority—but a minority often supported by European colonizers in central Africa. The accumulated hostility over generations revolved around a mix of fear, shame, and humiliation that led to efforts at genocide by the Hutus when colonial powers began to leave Central Africa. Hundreds of thousands of Tutsis were slaughtered by Hutus in the 1990s, as Hutu solidarity—often fueled by governmental actors—increased through the positive emotions felt in the arousal of righteous anger and need for revenge on those who had caused Hutu humiliation. Today in Uganda, it is the Tutsis who have attempted to kill off Hutus in order to maintain their power but also as vengeance for their losses in the 1990s. In other locations in Africa, similar dynamics are occurring.

Warfare

Wars occur for many geopolitical and geo-economic reasons that have little to do with the dynamics that I am emphasizing. Societies bump into each other as they expand, they compete for land, they need resources—in short, there are many causes of warfare. When wars are also fueled by high levels of negative emotional energy, they become more moral and more deadly because the dynamics that I am addressing begin to come into play. For example, the Franco–German conflicts between 1870 and 1945 have been viewed by Thomas Scheff (1994) as the result of both sides repressing their humiliation at losing various conflicts, only to come out as transmuted anger that kept warfare going. The rise of Nazi Germany is often seen as a consequence of the highly punitive terms imposed by the Allies on the Axis powers after World War I. Because the often-authoritarian culture of Germany (Prussia) at the turn of the 20th century, German had many elements of a shame culture—vestiges of which can be found today in Germany. It is hierarchical, and authority has historically been used to control others, often shaming them. But the reparations required of Germany at the end of World War I introduced a whole new level of collective humiliation that made the German people ready to extract revenge, against politically constructed (by the Nazi party) internal enemies like Jews and external enemies such as the rest of the Western world. Indeed, the Nazi party was originally more like a series of gangs, arousing prejudicial beliefs (common in Europe at the time) against Jews. A charismatic leader like Hitler consolidated the anger of Germans at their humiliation into true wartime atrocities, genocide toward the Jews of Germany, and efforts at conquest of all those nations that had humiliated Germans in World War I.

The U.S. invasion of Iraq can also be seen as involving some of these dynamics. The events of 9/11 not only brought fear to Americans but also a sense of humiliation that had never before been suffered (except, perhaps, in the American revolutionary war): extensive damage and loss of life by an external enemy on American soil, and moreover, a non-Christian enemy. The diffuse anger aroused by this humiliation and the public rituals displayed through the media only increased the sense that revenge *must be* extracted. If the war in Afghanistan was the only response, attributions would have been at least somewhat accurate, since 9/11 was orchestrated by Al Qaeda; here, at least, violence was leveled at the home base of an enemy that had been responsible for 9/11. The invasion of Iraq, however, demonstrates what can occur when attributions are incorrect because, for all the abuses of Saddam Hussein (often bordering on efforts at genocide of the Kurds), he was not involved in 9/11. The invasion was, as is all too obvious in retrospect, some combination of displaced anger and repressed shame transmuted into diffuse anger at Islam and its adherents that was fueled by an orchestrated campaign by the American government. As long as American nationalism could be charged up by demonization of "evil Muslim enemies," the war could be justified—despite the clearly flimsy evidence about "weapons of mass destructions." The result of the war was, as was the case in Yugoslavia, to remove the coercive force that had kept the three main ethnic subpopulations in Iraq from killing each other (with a genocidal intensity). The long-term consequence, I (along with many) would predict, will be another round of attempted genocide among the key ethnic/religious subpopulations once the American military vacates Iraq. Indeed, the re-partitioning of Iraq is a distinct possibility since it is not a "natural nation" but one constructed by England during its colonial period. But, the war effort in Iraq during its early days was widely supported by the American public because of their collective sense of anger at being attacked and, also, because of their sense of humiliation at the success of the attack by a ragtag group of terrorists.

Terrorism

Terrorism occurs when a subpopulation, often ethnic or religious in character, cannot successfully carry out full-blown warfare against a larger and/or more powerful population. By engaging in unpredictable violence against military, governmental, and civilian targets, terrorists can achieve their goal: to strike fear or terror and, hopefully in the end, to erode the power and solidarity of those on whom terror has been practiced. Like many forms of extreme violence, terrorism is often undertaken by those in a society who have been discriminated against and hence sanctioned negatively, and moreover, who have been unable to realize expectations in key institutional domains. Terrorism may remain confined to particular countries, as is the case with the conflict between Catholics and Protestants in Northern Ireland or between Basques and targets in Spain, but as is obvious, terrorism can also go global.

All terrorism is the result of members of a subpopulation feeling victimized by another, causing repression of shame and its transmutation into anger. International terrorism often exhibits, much like gang violence, the disconnection between people's actual sources of shame and the attributions that they make for the cause of this shame. Many of the actors in Al Qaeda are middle-class individuals from repressive but often oil-rich nations, such as Saudi Arabia. These individuals, it can be hypothesized, had experienced shame at their failures to move up corporate-unit hierarchies within domestic institutional domains. As they denied their shame or at least much of this shame, the cognitive connection to the actual causes of their sense of *humiliated fury*—domestic regimes of their own societies—was lost, and thus, they began to make more distal attributions to the West in general and American society in particular. Closer to home, they could also focus on Israel, which, in their eyes, continues to humiliate Arabs by its very presence. Individuals were helped along this path to inter-societal attributions by the media and propaganda machines of domestic leaders because distal attributions deflect attention away from the real source of shame: the existing structure and culture of terrorists' own societies of origin. The result has been all too clear, and the dynamics are very much like those for gang or genocidal collective actions but actions are enacted on a larger, global stage.

Terrorists organize into dense cells in which interaction rituals generate positive emotional arousal for thinking about and planning attacks on "enemies." The more positive emotions are ratcheted up, the more moral will the cause of terrorists become. And, the more they can make negative totems of their enemies, the more likely are they to sustain external attributions. Moreover, by collectively experiencing positive emotions when expressing negative emotions toward enemies, the solidarity of the cell rests not just on the positive emotional energy and symbols of the cell *per se*, but increasingly on the maintenance of a demonized enemy. When enemies are perceived as morally evil and as responsible for great harms, the internal solidarity of the cell becomes dependent upon sustaining this perception; and as positive emotions of interaction rituals in cells are mixed with negative emotions about enemies, the propensity for violence increases dramatically.

Social Movements

Social movements revolve around individuals becoming organized to change certain structural and cultural conditions in a society. Such movements tend to be focused on what are perceived to be wrongs that unfairly impose negative sanctions (often by virtue of discriminatory actions) and that prevent categories of persons from realizing reasonable expectations. Indeed, most social movements are caused by inequalities in a society, especially perceived injustices in the distribution of valued resources, including positive emotions. The shame and other negative emotions experienced by individuals can lead them to engage in confrontations with those in power that, at times, can become violent. But, most successful social movements evolve into an organizational phase, where the emotions experienced lead persons to seek resources—money, organizational structure, leaders, and allies—to focus collective action, which may be wholly peaceful in democratic societies or a combination of peaceful and violent in less democratic societies. The Civil Rights movement in the United States was mostly peaceful, with episodes of violence typically initiated by those working against the movement—a tactic that only brought allies to the movement and increased the solidarity among the corporate units spearheading the movement. The movement known as the Solidarity Movement in Poland during the 1980s before the collapse of the Soviet Union was also a mix of mostly peaceful but also some aggressive collective demonstrations, which often forced the repressive communist puppet state (of the Soviet Union) to engage in violent reprisals that only strengthened the appeal of the Solidarity Movement. At times, violence by members of Solidarity occurred but, more typically, protestors sought to damage the symbols of state power—thus killing totems more than real people. Here, in both the Civil Rights and Solidarity movements, the negative emotions remained more conscious, thus helping to sustain the focus on targets that were the actual sources of negative emotional experiences of individuals. The result was less violence than is often the case when shame and other negative emotions like fear are repressed, only to re-emerge as anger directed at distal targets that may not be the source of the problems experienced by those mobilizing.

Collective action cannot occur unless individuals are emotionally aroused and ready to mobilize. They must first have withdrawn emotional commitments to some institutional domains and their cultures, while deriving positive emotional energy from the very act of getting organized to vent negative emotions against perceived enemies. Other factors must also become part of the social movement—leadership, ideological codification of the problem and the solutions to the problem, administrative organization of the movement, recruitment of individuals to the movement, and financing of the movement (McCarthy and Zald 2001). What drives people to pull together all of these ingredients of social movements is a less volatile mix of negative emotions over conditions perceived to be unjust and positive emotions generated by "doing something" about injustices within cadres of protestors revealing relatively high degrees of solidarity.

Revolutions

Revolutions are violent collective actions that rather quickly cause the overthrow of an existing political regime in a society. There have, in actual fact, been relatively few true revolutions because many events called revolutions were initially unsuccessful efforts to overthrow a political regime that then evolved into longer-term civil wars where coercive forces of the regime and revolutionaries would organize and engage in traditional forms of warfare between armies. For example, the American, Chinese, Cuban, and Russian revolutions involved initial violence that was not successful in leading to a complete change of regimes in power; instead, the initial violence in the streets subsided as the participants retreated and re-organized as armies that would eventually win a sufficient number of battles to cause a change in the power structure of a society.

In contrast, the French, Iranian, and East German revolutions were more typical of this rare occurrence because collective street action, often violent, led to a rapid overthrow of the political regime. Revolutions can occur during the early stages of a social movement, where the negative emotions aroused by grievances of larger numbers of individuals lead to the emergence of leaders and to the early ideological codification of the injustices experienced by individuals but without the *high levels of organization* that eventually emerge in a social movement or in a civil war. Emotional arousal, intensified by a variety of leaders (often heads of differing factions) and by codification of emotions in ideologies outlining injustices, causes some individuals to take to the streets, often in the form of riots. But, because the intensity of negative emotions is so great and the number of people who have experienced these emotions is so large (at least relative to the population of urban areas where riots and revolutions are most likely to occur), the forces of social control are over-run or, as often happens, are induced by the rioters to join the demonstrators. Once these forces prove inadequate or shift allegiance, a revolution can run its course. Yet, at times, new centers of power intervene (well-organized religious leaders as in Iran or military leaders in a pre-emptive *coup d'état*) take over the revolutionary zeal of the population and re-direct the drive for change—often with the result of increasing potential for more violence down the road.

Revolutions, like all collective actions, are driven by emotions, those that withdraw commitments to institutional domains, such as polity, and those that mobilize individuals to incur the costs and risks of confronting centers of power. Thus, regimes live by the continued commitments of individuals to key institutional domains and their cultures, and they begin to die when these commitments are withdrawn by sufficiently large numbers of people or by powerful corporate actors. But until negative emotions among larger numbers of the general population lead them to the streets where they become even more emotionally energized by the collective propinquity, thereby charging up positive emotions for engagement against targets that have been negatively demonized, the true revolution cannot occur. The fact that revolutions are so rare indicates that these conditions are difficult to achieve in the right balance of incipient leadership and ideological formation, negative emotional arousal, some initial organization of individuals often in somewhat different factions, and willingness to take to the streets and confront centers of power. Most revolutions are crushed by the coercive forces of the state; others are co-opted before they begin or gather much steam; still others evolve into longer-term social movements or, if violence is needed, into factions in a more prolonged civil war involving full military mobilization by protestors.

Conclusion

It is important to recognize that changes in societies involving collective action and/ or violence have many causes and that the emotional dynamics involved are only *one* element—although a most critical one—in the events that unfold to alter the structure and culture of society. People often sustain commitments—that is, positive sentiments—toward the structures and cultures of both meso and macrostructures, with the result that social change must overcome this inertia. Yet, when large numbers of persons, especially those in categoric units such as social classes, ethnic subpopulations, religious sects, and other social categories, persistently experience negative emotions, these emotions can become a force for change in human societies. Changes typically come from a combination of withdrawal of positive emotions to existing sociocultural formations, coupled with the increasing arousal of negative emotions. As with most change-inducing negative emotion, its origins reside in emotional stratification, which has forced too many people to accumulate large reserves of negative emotional energy.

While negative emotional experiences can lead to behavioral and mental pathologies of individuals, to deviant acts by subgroups, or to focused violence between groups, these outcomes can typically be contained by the forces of social control in a society—unless these forces are very weak or do not enjoy widespread support by the general population. It is when negative emotions lead to coordinated actions that they can drive social change in a society, or even tear the society apart. Again, most of the time, the forces of social control win, at least in the short run. Yet, as negative emotions are aroused, collective outbursts such as riots or coordinated attacks by terrorist cells can occur; and over time these can lead to change-oriented social movements or to more violent efforts to change the structure and culture of a society. Just which way emotions are directed often depends upon conditions "on the ground" but, in general, violence increases when large numbers of individuals have consistently been shamed; and this situation is most likely to exist when a high level of inequality in the distribution of negative and positive emotions is evident in a society. The violence potential will increase to the degree that shame and sometimes guilt have been repressed, which can sever the connection between the real causes of emotional pain and the diffuse anger driving attributions about causes. Gangs represent the prototypical case where these dynamics have occurred because the anger is not generally directed at the individuals, corporate units, or even the institutional domains that have caused the shame that has been repressed.

What happens to gang members is more difficult to reproduce on a large scale. When large numbers of individuals have experienced shame, their anger and the attributions for this emotion typically remain somewhat conscious and accurate. But as acts of genocide and terrorism demonstrate, the sense of humiliation and the fury it generates can easily spin out of control, especially if leaders, media, and key corporate actors work to redirect that anger to targets not fully or, sometimes, only marginally responsible for the negative emotions that a subpopulation or members of a categoric unit or units have had to endure. When attributions are inaccurate and when negative emotions run high, the potential for violence is great, often manifesting itself in many different ways—riots, sectarian or forms of gang violence, guerrilla warfare, genocide, and other forms of highly volatile collective action.

What I have tried to argue and demonstrate with a few general examples is that societies are created and held together, at their core, by people's emotions. Indeed, a society is often a stand-off between emotions driving some to make commitments to the institutions of a society, while doing the opposite to others. There will never be a society that does not experience collective action, often very violent action, because humans are wired to be emotional. And so, there is no alternative to being human since this was the miracle that natural selection created: An evolved ape that could organize in difficult habitats and, when required, could build viable macro societies.

No other ape—indeed, no other mammal—has ever been able to achieve this level of social organization. Because of humans' emotionality, societies in very diverse and often problematic environments have been able to survive—albeit in a constant state of emotional tension in most cases. There is a "problem of emotions in human societies," as the title of this short monograph attests, but it is basic and fundamental to being human and, hence, this problem will never go away.

DISCUSSION QUESTIONS

1. Why is the problem with emotions in human societies inevitable and persistent?
2. What mixes of emotions increase the potential for violence in society, and why?
3. What difference does repression of negative emotions make in the form of either individual or collective action in a society?
4. How could societies realistically, and realism is the key here, be re-structured so as to reduce negative emotional arousal and, hence, the potential for violence?
5. Why is violence built into the human genome as it affects the wiring of the brain?

References

Barbalet, J. 1998. *Emotion, Social Theory, and Social Structure: A Macrosociological Approach*. Cambridge: Cambridge University Press.

Beck, A. 1999. *Prisoners of Hate: The Cognitive Basis of Anger, Hostility, and Violence*. New York: HarperCollins.

Berger, J. 1988. "Directions in Expectation States Research." Pp. 450–76 in *Status Generalization: New Theory and Research*, eds. M. Webster and M. Foschi. Stanford, CA: Stanford University Press.

Blau, P. M. 1977. *Inequality and Heterogeneity: A Primitive Theory of Social Structure*. New York: Free Press.

———. 1994. *Structural Context of Opportunities*. Chicago: University of Chicago Press.

Boehm, C. 1993. "Egalitarian Society and Reverse Dominance Hierarchy." *Current Anthropology 34*: 227–54.

Collins, R. 1975. *Conflict Sociology: Toward an Explanatory Science*. New York: Academic Press.

———. 2004. *Interaction Ritual Chains*. Princeton, NJ: Princeton University Press.

———. 2008. *Violence: A Micro-Sociological Theory*. Princeton, NJ: Princeton University Press.

Goffman, E. 1959. *The Presentation of Self in Everyday Life*. Garden City, NY: Anchor Books.

———. 1961. *Encounters: Two Studies in the Sociology of Interaction*. Indianapolis, IN: Bobbs-Merrill.

———. 1963. *Behavior in Public Places: Notes on the Social Organization of Gatherings*. New York: Free Press.

———. 1967. *Interaction Ritual*. Garden City, New York: Anchor Books.

———. 1971. *Relations in Public: Micro Studies of the Public Order*. New York: Basic Books.

———. 1981. *Forms of Talk*. Philadelphia: University of Pennsylvania Press.

———. 1983. "The Interaction Order." *American Sociological Review 48*: 1–17.

Heider, F. 1946. "Attitudes and Cognitive Organization." *Journal of Psychology 2*: 107–12.

———. 1958. *The Psychology of Interpersonal Relations*. New York: Wiley.

Lawler, E. J. 1992. "Affective Attachments to Nested Groups: A Choice-Process Theory." *American Sociological Review 57*: 327–36.

———. 1997. "Affective Attachments to Nested Groups: The Role of Rational Choice Processes." Pp. 387–403 in *Status, Network, and Structure*, eds. J. Szmatka, J. Skvoretz, and J. Berger. Stanford, CA: Stanford University Press.

———. 2001. "An Affect Theory of Social Exchange." *American Journal of Sociology 107*: 321–52.

Lawler, E. J., and S. R. Thye. 2006. "Social Exchange Theory of Emotion." Pp. 295–320 in *Handbook of the Sociology of Emotions*, eds. J. E. Stets and J. H. Turner. New York: Springer.

Lindner, Evelin. 2006. *Making Enemies: Humiliation and International Conflict*. London: Praeger Security International.

Luhmann, N. 1982. *The Differentiation of Society*. Translation by S. Holmes and C. Larmore. New York: Columbia University Press.

———. 1988. *Theory of Action: Towards a New Synthesis Going Beyond Parsons*. London: Routledge.

McCall, G. J., and J. L. Simmons. 1978. *Identities and Interactions*. New York: Free Press.

McCarthy, J., and M. Zald. 1977. "Resource Mobilization in Social Movements: A Partial Theory." *American Journal of Sociology 82*: 1212–39.

———. 2001. "Resource Mobilization Theory: Vigorous or Outmoded." Pp. 567–88 in *Handbook of Sociological Theory*, ed. J. H. Turner. New York: Kluwer Academic/Plenum.

Machalek, R. 1992. "Why are Large Societies Rare?" *Human Ecology 1*: 33–64.

Maryanski, A. 1992. "The Last Ancestor: An Ecological–Network Model on the Origins of Human Sociality." *Advances in Human Ecology 2*: 1–32.

———. 1993. "The Elementary Forms of the First Proto-Human Society: An Ecological/Social Network Approach." *Advances in Human Ecology*, volume 2. Greenwich, CT: JAI Press.

———. 1996a. "African Ape Social Networks: A Blueprint for Reconstructing Early Hominid Social Structure." Pp. 67–90 in *The Archaeology of Human Ancestry*, eds. J. Steele and S. Shennan. London: Routledge.

———. 1996b. "Was Speech an Evolutionary Afterthought?" Pp. 79–102 in *Communicating Meaning: The Evolution and Development of Language*, eds. B. Velichikovsky and D. Rumbaugh. Mahwah, NJ: Erlbaum.

———. 1997. "Primate Communication and the Ecology of a Language Niche." Pp. 191–209 in *Nonverbal Communication: Where Nature Meets Culture*, eds. U. Segerstrale and Peter Molnar. Hillsdale, NJ: Erlbaum.

Maryanski, A., and J. H. Turner. 1992. *The Social Cage: Human Nature and the Evolution of Society*. Stanford, CA: Stanford University Press.

Merton, R. K. 1938. "Social Structure and Anomie." *American Sociological Review 2*: 672–82.

Plutchik, R. 1962. *The Emotions: Facts, Theories, and a New Model*. New York: Random House.

———. 1980. *Emotion: A Psychoevolutionary Synthesis*. New York: Harper and Row.

Ridgeway, C. 1982. "Status Groups: The Importance of Motivation." *American Sociological Review 47*: 76–88.

———.1998. "Where Do Status Beliefs Come From?" Pp. 137–58 in *Status, Network, and Structure*, eds. J. Szmatka and J. Berger. Stanford, CA: Stanford University Press.

Ridgeway, C., E. Boyle, K. Kulpers, and D. Robinson. 1998. "How Do Status Beliefs Develop? The Role of Resources and Interaction." *American Sociological Review 63*: 331–50.

Ridgeway, C., and S. J. Correll. 2004. "Unpacking the Gender System: A Theoretical Perspective on Cultural Beliefs and Social Relations." *Gender and Society 18* (4): 510–31.

Ridgeway, C., and K. G. Erickson. 2000. "Creating and Spreading Status Beliefs." *American Journal of Sociology 106*: 579–615.

Ridgeway, C. L., and C. Johnson. 1990. "What is the Relationship Between Socioemotional Behavior and Status in Task Groups?" *American Journal of Sociology 95*: 1189–1212.

Ridgeway, C. L., and H. A. Walker. 1995. "Status Structure." Pp. 282–310 in *Sociological Perspectives on Social Psychology*, eds. K. S. Cook, G. A. Fine, and J. S. House. Boston: Allyn and Bacon.

Scheff, T. J. 1988. "Shame and Conformity: The Deference-Emotion System." *American Sociological Review 53*: 395–406.

———. 1994. *Bloody Revenge: Emotion, Nationalism and War*. Boulder, CO: Westview Press (reissued by Universe, 2000).

———. 1997. *Emotions, The Social Bond, and Human Reality*. New York: Cambridge University Press.

Scheff, T. J., and S. M. Retzinger. 1991. *Emotions and Violence: Shame and Rage in Destructive Conflicts*. Lexington, MA: Lexington Books.

Turner, J. H. 1984. *Societal Stratification: A Theoretical Analysis*. New York: Columbia University Press.

———. 1996a. "The Evolution of Emotions in Humans: A Darwinian–Durkheimian Analysis." *Journal for the Theory of Social Behaviour 26*: 1–34.

———. 1996b. "Cognition, Emotion and Interaction in the Big–Brained Primate." Pp. 295–315 in *Social Processes and Interpersonal Relations*, ed. K. M. Kwan. Greenwich, CT: JAI Press.

———. 1999. "The Neurology of Emotion: Implications for Sociological Theories of Interpersonal Behavior." Pp. 125–33 in *Mind, Brain, and Society: Toward a Neurosociology of Emotion*, eds. D. D. Franks and T. S. Smith. Stamford, CT: JAI Press.

———. 2000. *On the Origins of Human Emotions: A Sociological Inquiry Into the Evolution of Human Affect*. Stanford, CA: Stanford University Press.

———. 2007a. *Human Emotions: A Sociological Theory*. Oxford, UK: Routledge.

———. 2007b. "Justice and Emotions," *Social Justice Research 20*: 312–35.

———. 2007c. "The Social Psychology of Terrorism." Pp. 115–45 in *Understanding Terrorism*, ed. B. Phillips. Boulder, CO: Paradigm Press.

———. 2008. "Emotions and Social Structure: Toward a General Theory." Pp. 319–42 in *Emotions and Social Structure*, eds. D. Robinson and J. Clay-Warner. New York: Elsevier.

———. 2010a. *Principles of Sociology, Volume I on Macrodynamics*. New York, Springer.

———. 2010b. "The Stratification of Emotions: Some Preliminary Generalizations." *Sociological Inquiry 80*: 165–75.

Turner, J. H., and A. Maryanski. 2008. *On the Origin of Societies by Natural Selection*. Boulder, CO: Paradigm Press.

Turner, J. H., and D. Musick. 1985. *American Dilemmas: A Sociological Interpretation of Enduring Social Issues*. New York: Columbia University Press.

Turner, J. H., and J. E. Stets. 2005. *The Sociology of Emotions*. New York and Cambridge: University of Cambridge Press.

Turner, R. H. 2001. "Roles." Pp. 233–55 in *Handbook of Sociological Theory*, ed. J. H. Turner. New York: Plenum.

Volkan, V. D. 1988. *The Need to Have Hate*. Northvale, NJ: Aronson.

———. 1997. *Bloodlines: From Ethnic Pride to Ethnic Terrorism*. New York: Farrar, Straus and Giroux.

———. 2004. *Blind Trust: Large Groups and their Leaders in Times of Crisis and Terror*. Charlottesville, VA: Pitchstone.

Williams, Jr., R. M. 1970. *American Society*. New York: Knopf.

Glossary/Index

Note: Page numbers followed by "f" refer to figures and followed by "t" refer to tables.

attribution, processes of (*continued*)
  and gang violence 52
  self-attribution 15, 39, 46, 47
aversion–fear 4t, 5, 6t, 8, 8t

B
behavioral pathologies 43–45, 46
brain, emotional wiring in 4, 6, 10, 11, 44

C
categoric unit(s): social units or categories within a society, often differentially val-
    ued and treated by others 16, 32–33, 33–34, 48–49
  Civil Rights movement 46, 57–58
  class
    stratification of 24, 30–31
    and unequal distribution of emotional energy ix–x, 25, 37–38, 41, 45–46
collective actions 39, 50–59
  feuds 51
  and force for change in society 59–60
  gang violence 51–53, 60
  genocide 53–54, 60
  revolutions 58–59
  social movements 57–58
  terrorism 17, 55, 56–57, 60
  warfare 55–56
corporate units: social units that are constructed by forming a division of labor
    devoted to realizing particular goals 16, 26–29, 30, 48
culture, vertical integration of 38, 39f

D
defense mechanism(s): the movement of unpleasant and painful experiences arous-
    ing negative emotions about self out of conscious awareness 12–15, 46–47
defensive strategies: cognitive–interpersonal techniques to enable a person to escape
    negative emotions aroused by negative sanctions by others 12–13
depression 7, 9, 45, 46
disappointment–sadness 4t, 6t, 7, 8, 8t, 9
disavowals 12
disgust 3
displacement 13–14
distal bias (of attributions): individuals make external attributions about the causes

as residing in remote others, categories of others, and social structures (and their cultures) 16–18, 18–19, 36, 47
domestic violence 47

E
embarrassment 6, 7
emotional arousal
    attribution processes extending reach of 17
    basic conditions of 18–19, 23
    in encounters 33–34
    of guilt 7, 38, 39, 44, 46
    of negative emotions 18–19, 20, 22, 23, 33–35, 44, 46
    of positive emotions 18, 19, 22
    role of identities in 20–22, 21f, 23, 32
    and sanctions 7, 18–19, 23, 33, 44, 46
emotional energy
    and commitment to macrostructures of society 36, 42
    mixing of positive and negative 48–49, 52–53, 55, 57, 58
    organization of 49–50
    and stratification of emotions 35–38
    unequal distribution of ix–x, 25, 37–38, 41, 45–46
ethnicity 16, 32, 33, 41, 46, 48, 53
expectancy 3
expectations 18–19
    arousal of negative emotions and failure to meet 18, 22, 23, 33, 44, 46
    attribution processes in failure to realize 39–40, 50
    downwards adjustment of 37–38
    of identity 22, 23
    meeting or exceeding of 18–19, 35
    stratification of emotions and rising 38–41

F
fear 3, 5, 8–9, 10, 14t, 35
    aversion–fear 4t, 5, 6t, 8, 8t
    collective 54, 55, 56
    gender dynamic in 50
    in response to repressed guilt 9, 45
    and self-attribution 39
feuds 51
first-order elaborations (of emotions): the mixing of one primary emotion with a lesser amount of another primary emotion 4–6, 6t, 10

focused encounter: face-to-face interaction among individuals in which their bodies are aligned for communication, mutual focus of attention, arousal of emotions, and solidarity 33, 34

G

gang violence 51–53, 60

generalized symbolic media of exchange: symbols marking value and also used by individuals in exchanges within and between institutional domains 27–30, 28t, 31, 38, 41–42

genocide 53–54, 60

gratitude 5

guilt: a second-order negative emotion combining sadness, fear, and anger that is aroused when individuals feel that they have violated moral codes 6, 7, 8, 8t, 9

    arousal of 7, 38, 39, 44, 46

    attributions to avoid 15–16

    collective 9, 11, 45–46

    and increased potential for behavioral pathologies 44–45

    repressed 7, 9, 11, 14t, 18, 40, 45, 60

    self-attributions of 46

H

happiness 3, 5, 7, 10

    satisfaction–happiness 3, 4t, 5, 6t, 35

hominids/hominins: extinct primates that evolved from apes and are believed to be on the human line, or close to the human line (or clade) of evolution 1

hopefulness 5

humiliated fury 44, 47, 56, 60

humiliation 6, 46, 50

    collective 51, 54, 55–56

    from sanctions 46

    fuelling violence 44, 46

I

identity/identities: cognitive/emotional constructions that persons develop about themselves in all social contexts 20

    of gang members 52–53

    on the line 18, 19, 23, 35, 37, 41, 44

    role in emotional arousal 20–22, 21f, 23, 32

ideology/ideologies: systems of highly evaluative beliefs built from generalized symbolic media 30, 38, 39, 39f

institutional domain(s): congeries and sets of corporate units that address particular problems of human populations' environments 16, 25–30, 31, 36, 41–42

institutional norm(s): within a given institutional domain, the appropriate and excepted behaviors of individuals and actions of corporate units 38

Iraq
    possible future for 56
    U.S. invasion of 49–50, 55–56

Israel 17, 39, 56

J

jealousy 5

M

meta-ideology: the composite ideology that emerges in a society when the ideologies of each institutional domain are combined 31, 33, 34, 36, 38, 39f

mobility rates 24

mobilization of resources 50

monkeys 2

moral codes 7, 8, 38, 46
    guilt and violation of 7, 38, 39, 44

N

natural selection 2, 5, 6, 8, 10

Nazi Germany 53, 55

negative emotions 5–9, 10
    accumulating negative emotional energy 35–38
    arousals of 18–19, 20, 22, 23, 33–35, 44, 46
    attributions extending reach of 15–18
    collective action to vent 59–60
    defense mechanisms to protect self from 12–15, 46–47
    mixing of positive and negative emotional energy 48–49, 52–53, 55, 57, 58
    repression of 11, 23, 40, 41

O

origins of emotions 1–3

P

Palestinian plight 49–50

positive emotions 3
    arousal of 18, 19, 22
    becoming more distal 18–19, 36

positive emotions (*continued*)

    mixing of positive and negative emotional energy 48–49, 50, 52–53, 57, 58

    proximal bias of 16, 17–18

    securing resources and increasing positive emotional energy 35–36

pride 5, 6t, 7, 35

primary emotions: emotions that are hard-wired in the brain and that humans and mammals all share 3–4, 4t

projection 14

proximal bias (of attributions): the tendency of the arousal of positive emotions to be attributed to the actions of self or to others in the local encounter 16, 17–18

R

range of emotions 3–9

reaction-formation 15

relief 5, 6t

religious affiliations 16, 20, 32, 33, 48, 53

repression: the neurological process whereby experiences tagged with negative emotions are pushed into the subcortical areas of the brain, and hence, out of a person's conscious awareness 11, 23

    and attribution processes 15–18

    and defense mechanisms for 12–15, 46–47

    gender dynamic in 50

    of guilt 7, 9, 11, 14t, 18, 40, 45, 60

    and increased potential for behavioral pathologies 44–45

    increasing intensity of emotion 19, 46–47

    of shame 7, 9, 17, 40, 41, 44–45, 56, 58

resource mobilization 50

reverence 5, 6t

revolutions 58–59

righteous anger 7, 51, 54

Rwanda 53, 54

S

sadness 3, 7, 8, 9, 10, 35

    avoidance of 15

    disappointment–sadness 4t, 6t, 7, 8, 8t, 9

    in response to repressed guilt and shame 9, 45

    and self-attribution 39, 46

sanctions

    and emotional arousal 7, 18–19, 23, 33, 44, 46

    in encounters with corporate units 35, 39, 40, 44

gang membership and positive 52–53

satisfaction–happiness 3, 4t, 5, 6t, 35

second-order elaborations (of emotions): three negative primary emotions are combined to produce such emotions as shame, guilt, and alienation 6–8, 10

secondary defense mechanisms: those defense mechanisms that involve repression of negative emotions, coupled with another type of defense mechanism that further represses the negative emotions, often intensifying the emotions and transmuting them to new types of negative emotion 12, 13–15, 14t, 23

selective interpretation 12

selective perception 12

Serbs 54

shame: a second-order negative emotion generated by mixing sadness, anger, and fear resulting in a feeling of incompetence in meeting situational expectation 6–7, 8–9, 8t

　　and "ashamed of being ashamed" cycle 16, 46

　　collective 9, 11, 45–46, 51, 55, 58, 60

　　in failure to realize expectations 38

　　gender dynamic in repressing 50

　　and increased potential for behavioral pathologies 44–45

　　and links to violence 9, 47, 60

　　repressed 7, 9, 17, 40, 41, 44–45, 56, 58

short-term credit 12–13

social bonding

　　emotions to promote organization and 2, 5, 8

　　obstacle of negative 3, 10

social movements 57–58

society

　　collective anger and danger to 45–50

　　distal bias for negative emotions a problem to 17–18

　　feuds in 51

　　gang violence in 51–53

　　genocide 53–54, 60

　　organization of 25–35

　　problems of unverified identities 22

　　revolutions 58–59

　　social movements 57–58

　　stratification and tensions in 31, 32, 34, 45–46

　　terrorism 17, 55, 56–57, 60

　　values of American 38, 40–41, 40t

　　warfare in 55–56

Solidarity Movement, Poland 57–58

standards of justice: social beliefs about the appropriate level of rewards that individuals should receive, based upon their costs and investments incurred compared with the cost, investments, rewards of others in the same type of situation 41

status beliefs: beliefs that individuals in a society hold about the qualities and characteristics of members of categoric units and that are used to make moral evaluations of their worth and to develop expectations for their behaviors 33–34

stratification: a macrostructure of classes, rank-ordering and mobility between classes created by virtue of the unequal distribution of valued resources 16, 22, 23

T

U

unfocused encounter: interaction in public places where, for example, individuals monitor each other's movements and memberships in categoric units, without making face-engagement and thereby focusing the encounter 34

V

values: society-wide, abstract standards of good–bad, right–wrong, etc. 19, 38

University Readers™
Reading Materials Evolved.

Introducing the

SOCIAL ISSUES COLLECTION

A Routledge/University Readers Custom Library for Teaching

Customizing course material for innovative and excellent teaching in sociology has never been easier or more effective!

Choose from a collection of more than 300 readings from Routledge, Taylor & Francis, and other publishers to make a custom anthology that suits the needs of your social problems/ social inequality, and social issues courses.

All readings have been aptly chosen by academic editors and our authors and organized by topic and author.

Online tool makes it easy for busy instructors:

1. Simply select your favorite Routledge and Taylor & Francis readings, and add any other required course material, including your own.

2. Choose the order of the readings, pick a binding, and customize a cover.

3. One click will post your materials for students to buy. They can purchase print or digital packs, and we ship direct to their door within two weeks of ordering!

More information at www.socialissuescollection.com

Contact information: Call your Routledge sales rep, or
Becky Smith at University Readers, 800-200-3908 ext. 18, bsmith@universityreaders.com
Steve Rutter at Routledge, 207-434-2102, Steve.Rutter@taylorandfrancis.com.

Routledge
Taylor & Francis Group
an **informa** business

3764裊2